PROVINCIAL POLITICS
AND THE
PAKISTAN MOVEMENT

The Growth of The Muslim League in
North-West and North-East India 1937-47

PROVINCIAL POLITICS
AND THE
PAKISTAN MOVEMENT

The Growth of The Muslim League in
North-West and North-East India 1937-47

IAN TALBOT

KARACHI
OXFORD UNIVERSITY PRESS
OXFORD   NEW YORK   DELHI
1988

Oxford University Press

OXFORD NEW YORK
TORONTO MELBOURNE AUCKLAND
PETALING JAYA SINGAPORE HONG KONG TOKYO
DELHI BOMBAY CALCUTTA MADRAS KARACHI
NAIROBI DAR ES SALAAM CAPE TOWN

and associates in

BERLIN IBADAN

Oxford is a trademark of Oxford University Press

First Edition, 1988

ISBN 0 19 577387 X

Printed by
Civil & Military Press (Pvt) Ltd.
Published by
Oxford University Press
5-Bangalore Town Sharae Faisal
P.O.Box 13033, Karachi-8, Pakistan.

To Lois

To Lois

Contents

Abbreviations

The following abbreviations are used in the notes to the text.

FMA	Freedom Movement Archives (Karachi University)
IOL	India Office Library
IOR	India Office Records
FR	Fortnightly Report
SHC	Shamsul Hasan Collection
QIAP	Quaid-i-Azam Papers
NAI	National Archives of India

Preface

This short study sets out to widen our knowledge concerning the making of Pakistan. Existing works have increased our understanding of the events and issues at stake at the All-India level which led to its creation. Jinnah's skilful playing of the Muslim card during the Second World War, has, for example, been carefully explored. Much less has been written, however, about political developments in the Muslim provinces during the decade which preceded Partition. The demand for a separate Muslim state arose, it is true, outside of the majority areas. Yet its ultimate success depended on the support received from these regions.

Provincial Politics and the Pakistan Movement aims to reveal how the Muslim League overcame its earlier weakness in the major centres of Muslim population and swung them behind its demand for Pakistan. The answers it gives will also shed light on the freedom movement's legacy and the role of Islam in politics during the crucial period of 1937-47.

This treatise has emerged out of a number of years study of the Muslim League Movement and the demand for Pakistan. During this period I have incurred many debts of gratitude. My greatest debt is to Dr. Francis Robinson, my research supervisor, whose sound advice has been a continuous source of assistance. His own exacting standards have helped me avoid many errors of style.

I would also like to thank the Arts' Deans of the University of Sussex for supporting me with an overseas travel grant in the summer of 1986. This enabled me to visit Pakistan again, during the closing stages of preparing the manuscript. In Pakistan I have received much encouragement and advice from a number of people. These include, Professor Sharif

Al Mujahid of the Quaid-i-Azam Academy, the Director and Staff of the National Archives of Pakistan, in Islamabad, and Professor M.H. Siddiqi and his Staff at the Freedom Movement Archives at Karachi University. I must especially thank, however, Khalid Shamsul Hasan for the permission to consult his father's fine private collection and for the trouble he has taken in helping me with my research and for his friendship and gracious hospitality.

I am also grateful to the Librarian and Staff of the National Archives of India and of the Nehru Memorial Museum and Library for their courteous assistance. Thanks also go to Professor Mushirul Hasan of Jamia Millia Islamia, for his unfailing support during my visits to New Delhi.

I am much obliged for the work of the Librarians and Staff Museum in London. Finally, I am grateful for the comments of numerous colleagues over the years. Any errors of fact or omissions are my responsibility alone.

University of Sussex   IAN TALBOT
December 1987

Introduction

On the eve of the British departure from India some eighty
million Muslims lived in the subcontinent[1] forming about a
quarter of the total population. In central and southern India
the Muslims were in a tiny minority. But in the north-west
and north-east they had a majority over other communities.
Indeed, the two regions of Bengal and Punjab between them
contained over 60 per cent of the Indian Muslim population.
The centres of Muslim population varied considerably, however, in their natural setting and economic and social structure. There could hardly be a greater contrast between the
sparsely populated tribal society of the North-West Frontier
Province and the teeming peasant populations of the delta
districts of Bengal. Even within the majority provinces themselves, there were immense variations. The most striking were
the existence of extensive tracts of non-Muslim majority
populations within West Bengal and East Punjab.[2] This feature in the main centres of Muslim population led eventually
to Punjab and Bengal being sliced in two when Pakistan was
created.

The demand for Pakistan[3] was first voiced by the All-India
Muslim League at its annual session at Lahore in March 1940.
Its success required the politicians and voters from the
centres of Muslim population to come under the League's
banner and thus provide its President, Mohammed Ali Jinnah
with a secure mandate in his negotiations with the Congress
and the British. The League had traditionally, however,
wielded little influence in the Muslim majority areas. Although
it claimed from the time of its formation in 1906 to represent the whole of the Indian Muslim community, it was in
reality, for most of that period, the vehicle of the educated

and landed Muslim minority of the United Provinces. This group had traditionally exercised political power before the advent of British rule. When the British began to devolve power from the late 1880s onwards, it became increasingly aware that without constitutional safeguards it would be elbowed to one side by the majority Hindu community in the race for the control of local power and patronage. The Muslim League was formed primarily to secure such protection. Its United Provinces' controllers' conveniently glossed over the fact that the interests of the Muslim majority areas of India might not correspond with their own.

The first conflict arose at the time of the *Lucknow Pact of 1916* between the All-India Muslim League and the Indian National Congress. This agreement over the quota of Muslim seats for future representation in the Legislatures was concluded by the League on behalf of Muslim India. In fact, it represented the sectional interests of the UP and one particular clique within its Muslim politics; the 'Young Muslim' Party which with the support of the *ulema* (priests) had temporarily wrested control of the League organization from the Conservative landowners. The Pact significantly favoured the United Provinces' interests to the detriment of those of the Muslim majority areas. The United Provinces where Muslims made up just 14 per cent of the population had 50 per cent of the legislative seats reserved for Muslims, whereas in Bengal, the Muslim majority of 52 per cent was allocated just 40 per cent of the seats, whilst in Punjab the Muslim majority of 54 per cent had to be content with 50 per cent of the seats.

In the late 1920s the interests of the Muslim provinces and the minority areas again came into collision. Jinnah in his discussions with Motilal Nehru showed he was prepared to bargain away separate electorates which worked to the majority areas' advantage in return for concessions to the Muslims in a future responsible Central Assembly. Further evidence that the All-India Muslim League had little to offer the Punjabi or Bengali Muslims came from its own constitution.

Punjab, although it had double the United Provinces' Muslim population, had only the same number of seats on the League's Council.[4]

The Muslim League's neglect of the major centres of Muslim population increasingly became a handicap, as the British devolved more power to the provinces. The *Montagu-Chelmsford Reforms, 1919* transferred control of certain 'nation-building' subjects of administration such as local self-government and education to ministers responsible to a provincial council. A situation was thus created in which the previous political backwaters of the majority areas became important centres of Muslim power and influence. Muslim regional parties such as the Punjab Unionists shut out the Muslim League from this power. In its own United Provinces and Bombay heartland, it had to be content with the crumbs which fell from the Congress table. For the time being its role was limited to mediating between the regional Muslim groups, the British and the Congress. This proved so frustrating and limiting that by 1930 Jinnah had abandoned it and retired to England. In his absence, the Muslim League became virtually moribund.

The passage of the *Government of India Act, 1935* with its introduction of Provincial Autonomy and plans for a Federal Legislature on which Princely India would be represented, encouraged Jinnah to try once again. He returned to India to organize the Muslim League to fight the Assembly elections which were to be held throughout India's provinces early in 1937. The results reflected the Muslim League's historic lack of influence in the Muslim majority areas. Whilst it won 20 of the 39 Muslim seats in Bombay and 27 of the 64 United Provinces' Muslim seats, in Punjab it captured just one of the 86 Muslim constituencies. In the North-West Frontier Province and Sind it had no success at all. The only relatively bright spot was Bengal where it won 39 of the 119 seats reserved for Muslims. This was the only majority area where the League had any influence in the countryside.

Bitterness at being excluded from power-sharing in the United Provinces, together with the 'oppression'[5] of the Congress ministries in seven of India's eleven provinces led the League to take up the idea for a Muslim state. As early as 1930 the Punjabi poet-politician, Muhammed Iqbal, had stated in his Presidential Address at the Muslim League session at Allahabad that he would like to see 'the Punjab, North-West Frontier Province, Sind, and Baluchistan amalgamated into a single state'. In January 1933, Chaudhuri Rahmat Ali, a Cambridge law student, put forward a scheme for a fully independent territorial Muslim State in a pamphlet entitled *Now Or Never*. It coined the term Pakistan—land of the pure—for the first time, the name coming from the five Muslim northern units of India, Punjab, North-West Frontier Province—Afghan Province, Kashmir, Sind and Baluchistan. During 1938-9 a number of 'Pakistan Schemes' were put forward—the *Lahore Resolution of 23 March 1940* emerged from them. It was deliberately left vague[6] in its territorial definition in order to leave Jinnah room for manoeuvre, and to provide a rallying call for Muslims from both the minority and majority areas. The League faced an uphill struggle to 'sell' the idea to the majority areas' politicians. They did not feel so threatened by the Hindu and Sikh communities as did their brethren elsewhere in India. In the case of the Punjab Unionists their interests were tied up in co-operation with these groups. As early as September 1940, the Unionist Premier, Sikander, declared that the *Lahore Resolution* did not contemplate any division of India. The Muslim Premier of Sind, Hidayatullah, remained similarly sceptical about the Pakistan Scheme. The Muslim League had somehow to either win over such opponents or push them to one side, if its demand was to appear credible. It would never be seriously listened to by the British or the Congress if it had no influence in the areas it was claiming for Pakistan. The League backed up its rhetoric at the ballot box in the 1946 Provincial Elections. Less than a decade after its debacle in the majority areas, it turned the tables on its opponents. In Punjab, it captured 75 of the Muslim seats, in Bengal 115, in Sind 30. Throughout India it secured 75 per cent of the total Muslim vote in comparison with its 4.4 per cent in 1937. Jinnah had been given the mandate for Pakistan. How had this remarkable transformation come about?

This is the central theme of this book. It is a largely unexplored area. Most studies of the Pakistan Movement have concentrated either on the Muslim cultural homeland of the United Provinces[7] where the Muslim League gained its earliest foothold, or on the All-India negotiations between Jinnah, the Congress, and the British.[8] Those explanations which have been advanced to understand the Muslim League's advance in the 'Pakistan areas' lack conviction. Penderel Moon, an ex-ICS man in the Punjab, simply attributes this to the alluring and irresistible appeal of the Pakistan cry to the Muslim masses.[9] We need to know, however, what they understood by Pakistan and how this cry was communicated to them, before we move beyond the realm of generalities. Peter Hardy's suggestion that the Muslim League gained its electoral success in the Punjab by making an appeal over the heads of the professional politicians[10] raises more questions than it solves. For instance, how did the League bypass the traditional holders of power? And how can this explanation be reconciled with the fact that the majority of the League's candidates in 1946 were experienced politicians who had only very recently switched their allegiance to it. Pakistani historians have largely explained the League's success in terms of the Two Nation Theory which is that the Indian Muslims had always constituted a separate nation,[11] awaiting only to be organized and inspired by the Muslim League to assert this fact. But how similar were the cultural outlooks of Bengali, Pushtu, Punjabi, and Sindhi speakers? Moreover, why was the League such a latecomer to the majority areas, where according to the Two Nation Theory, Muslims' separate development and national awareness ought to have been most clearly defined?

Recently, the American political scientist, Paul Brass, has developed another theory for understanding Muslim separatism in North India.[12] He argues that the League grew there, because there was both an elite which chose to manipulate separatist symbols in order to serve its own power interests and a socially mobilized Muslim community[13] which responded to the sense of communal identification communicated to it. This argument, whether or not it works in the United Provinces, which seems doubtful, fails to explain the League's success in the backward areas of rural Sind, Punjab, Bengal, and the Frontier.

This work sets out to shed fresh light on the League's growth in the Muslim majority areas of India during the decade which preceded the creation of Pakistan. It will focus on political developments in the Muslim provinces, although these will be set in the context of the changing situation at the national level of politics. Key areas of concern will be the Muslim League's organizational structure and its mobilization of political support. Chapter 1 examines the Muslim League's position in the North-West Frontier Province. Although its Muslim population numbered less than three quarters of a million its adherence to the Pakistan Scheme was of vital strategic importance, as well as of symbolic significance in the light of the Congress' long established influence in the region. Chapter 2 analyses the Muslim League's development in Sind. Three million Muslims lived in Sind which was newly created as a Muslim majority province in 1936. Chapter 3 assesses the Muslim League's situation in Bengal, the most populous area of Muslim India with over 33 million followers of Islam. Bengal had not been included in the 'Pakistan Schemes' of Rahmat Ali and Iqbal, but the *Lahore Resolution* had referred to a Muslim state in north-east India. Finally Chapter 4 examines the Muslim League's growth in Punjab. This was the key province for the success of the Pakistan demand. There could be no separate Muslim State without it. Yet the Muslim League had always faced difficulties in the region. The

Punjab Muslim League was disaffiliated in 1916 and then again in 1929, after differences with its parent organization. By the latter date, the League was virtually irrelevant in Punjab politics because of the predominance of the Unionist Party. Its founder, Mian Fazl-i-Husain, used this as a springboard to challenge the League at the All-India level, through the All-India Muslim Conference. In such unfavourable circumstances, the Punjab League struggled to survive during the early 1930s, although it had Iqbal as one of its leading figures.

Despite the variety of material and economic settings, the Muslim League faced a similar political task in each of the majority areas. It had to spread its influence from the towns into the countryside where the bulk of the voters resided.[14] The rural Muslim population were educationally backward. Their outlook was a complex interplay of awareness of Islamic community (asbiyyat) and allegiance to tribal and clan loyalties. Their religious experience was centred on the 'folk' Islam of the Sufi shrine, rather than on the faith of the Book and the mosque. The Muslim League's success depended on its ability to present its appeal in this rural idiom. For only by doing so could it be made intelligible to the villagers who held the key to the creation of Pakistan.

REFERENCE

1. In addition to the 80 million in British India, 15 million lived in the Princely States.
2. See *Appendix B* for details.
3. Or to be strictly accurate for independent Muslim States in the north-west and north-east of India.
4. Sind and the North-West Frontier Province between them only had half the seats allocated to Bombay.
5. The *Shareef* and *Pirpur Reports* luridly highlighted allegations of government attempts to 'Hinduize' the Muslims through educational reforms, to force cow-protection on them, and to force Muslims to sing the 'Bande Mataram'. Whether or not all these allegations were justified, they were believed.
6. It did not, of course, contemplate the partition of Punjab or Bengal.
7. Robinson, F., *Separatism Among Indian Muslims : The Politics of the United Provinces' Muslims 1860-1923*, Cambridge, 1976.
8. Ayesha Jalal's recent work, *The Sole Spokesman*, Cambridge, 1985 uneasily straddled the different political worlds of New Delhi and the Provinces. The centre of her focus, however, remains the All-India level of politics.

9. Moon, P., *Divide and Quit*, London, 1963, p.41.
10. Hardy, P., *The Muslims of British India*, Cambridge, 1973, p.238.
11. K.B. Sayeed in a classic exposition of the Two Nations Theory declared: 'There has never taken place a confluence of the two civilizations in India—the Hindu and the Muslim—they may have meandered towards each other here and there, but on the whole the two have flowed their separate courses—sometimes parallel and sometimes contrary to one another'. Sayeed, K.B., *Pakistan : The Formative Phase 1857-1948*, London, 1968, p.12.
12. Brass, P., *Language, Religion and Politics in North India*, Cambridge, 1974, p.178 and ff.
13. By social mobilization, Brass means an urbanized, literate community which can look beyond the narrow confines of the 'traditional' village.
14. In Punjab, for example, in only six of the 29 districts did more than a fifth of the Muslims live in towns. It should also be noted that the franchise was still limited in 1946—only 11 per cent of Punjab's Muslims were enfranchised, in Sind the figure was 22 per cent, in the Frontier Province 16 per cent, and in Bengal 14 per cent.

1

The Troublesome Frontier

The North-West Frontier Province's location[1] made it crucial
to the Muslim League's plans for a separate state which was
strategically tenable. Yet, even though it contained a higher
percentage of Muslims than any other province in India, it
remained a centre of Congress influence until the final
months before Partition. Although a Muslim League ministry
had been in office from October 1943 to March 1945, the
League in stark contrast to its showing elsewhere in India,
fared poorly in the 1946 Frontier elections. It won a mere 17
seats to the Congress's 30. This result undoubtedly hampered
the Muslim League in its national bargaining position *vis-a-vis*
the Congress and the British. It also ensured that the
Frontier's fate would be decided by external events and negotiations.

The independence movement in the Frontier arouses a
whole range of questions. Why was it the only province in
which the Congress seriously competed for Muslim loyalties?
What prevented the Muslim League from capitalizing on its
period in office? What lay behind the Muslim League's
dramatic improvement in fortune between the 1946 Provincial Elections and its successful June 1947 Referendum Campaign for Pakistan? How strong was the Muslim League organization in the region on the eve of Partition? Before
attempting to answer these questions, however, it is first
necessary to examine those features of the Frontier's history,
economic, and social life which affected its political development during the final decade of British rule.

THE FRAMEWORK OF PRE-INDEPENDENCE POLITICS

The Frontier Province's rural character; the composition of
its population; the influence of the Pathan social code and

factional politics; the importance of *Pirs* in Frontier society; and the existence of anti-British feeling amongst important segments of the population following the 23 April 1930 riots in Peshawar and the subsequent disobedience campaigns, together provided the framework for Muslim politics in the region. The Muslim League's slow development in the Frontier can only be fully understood within this context. It is, therefore, necessary to examine each of these five influences in turn.

(a) *The North-West Frontier Province's Rural Character.* The North-West Frontier Province was overwhelmingly a rural area. The *1931 Census* estimated that just 16 per cent of its population lived in towns.[2] Moreover, many of these were little more than glorified villages. Peshawar city itself was not an industrial centre, but rather an administrative and market centre. One reason for the lack of urban development was that considerable areas of the region did not have a high enough agricultural base to support a large population.[3] Equally important, however, was the hostility to town life of the Frontier's dominant ethnic group, the Pathans. The Pathans traditionally believed that agriculture and warfare were the only honourable occupations. Urban lifestyles were degrading and inferior to their own tribal mores. Those towns which existed by the twentieth century owed their development largely to Muslim immigrants from other provinces and to the minority Hindu and Sikh population.[4] Two important consequences stemmed from the province's urban development. Firstly, there was an immense cultural divide between the towns and the surrounding Pathan rural areas. Secondly, the political influence of the urban population counted for very little. Traditionally non-Pathans were able to play only a subordinate role in Frontier politics and society. When elective politics began to be introduced by the British, the urban classes lacked sufficient numbers to increase their influence.

(b) *The Province's Ethnic and Cultural Composition.* The main ethnic division was between the Pathans and other groups. Whilst the Pathans predominated in the surrounding tribal territories, they were in fact in a minority in the Frontier Province itself. Non-Pathan Muslims formed 55 per cent of the population, Hindus and Sikhs 8 per cent, and the Pathans 37 per cent. The Pathans and Muslim non-Pathans were not, however, evenly distributed throughout the Province. In Peshawar, Kohat, and Bannu, Pathans formed a clear majority of the population. Hazara and Dera Ismail Khan were marked off from these areas, as here non-Pathan Muslims dominated. The ethnic composition of the latter regions reflected the fact that they were geographically cut off from the remainder of the N.W.F.P., and were oriented towards the Punjab. This was to have important political consequences during the period of the Pakistan Movement. The smallness of the Hindu and Sikh community and its virtual invisibility in the centres of Pathan culture and population also had important political repercussions. For whilst other Muslims might view them as a threat to their religion and culture, so far as the Pathans were concerned it was inconceivable and laughable that they might be ruled by Hindus.

Although the Pathans formed less than two-fifths of the population, they were its ascendant ethnic group. They not only possessed a cultural homogenity the non-Pathan Muslims lacked, but more importantly for centuries they had wielded political and social power in the Frontier.[5] They remained the dominant political grouping down to the end of British rule. The aim of all political organizations within the region was thus to secure Pathan support, without it they would be confined to the margins of Frontier society.

(c) *Pathan Society.* Pathans trace descent through the male line to a common putative ancestor named *Qais.* He lived at the time of the Prophet according to their legends and was converted to Islam by him.[6] Pathan social organization is structured around patrilineal descent groups descending progressively from tribe, clan, sub-clan, and section. Descent also determines land ownership and distribution, a tribe's land being permanently divided amongst its smaller descent groups. Over time the land system became less egalitarian, as the periodical redistribution of land—*vesh*—was abandoned. Nevertheless, all Pathans were entitled to a share *'daftar'* of his lineage's estate. Political rights—the right to participate in the tribal councils—*jirgas*—accompanied this entitlement. Non-Pathans on the other hand, who owned no land, were excluded from the deliberations. They had neither economic nor political independence, and in pre-British times, they were completely subservient to the Pathan landed elite, who acted as their protectors and employers. Even on the eve of Independence, few non-Pathan artisans or tenants would dare to oppose the political wishes of their Pathan patron.

Pathan politics traditionally revolved around factional rivalry amongst landholders—'parajamba'. The most vital aspect of this, was competition among patrilineal cousins *'taburwali'* (*'tabur'* in Pushtu means first cousin). *'Taburs'* organized factions *'gundis'* consisting of their lineage segment and clients in their struggle for political prominence or land. Faction leaders of lesser stature were known as *'Maliks'*. More important faction leaders who, moreover, displayed the qualities on which Pathans placed a high value (bravery, hospitality, a reputation for defending his honour) were designated as Khans.[7]

What is of crucial importance for an understanding of Frontier politics is the fact that this traditional *'taburwali'* system not only survived down to the 1940s but formed the basis on which such parties as the Congress and the Muslim League extended their influence into the countryside. Factions offered them a means of tying in their appeal to a familiar and vital political system. The cost of intermingling *taburwali* with party politics was, however, that if one local faction joined the Muslim League its traditional rival would join the Congress and vice versa. Political alignments thus frequently reflected the underlying divisions within Pathan society and had little to do with the cause a Khan and his followers supported.

(d) *The Pirs of the Frontier*. The *Pirs* of the Frontier are venerated as elsewhere in the Muslim world because of the belief that they have inherited the spiritual powers of their saintly ancestors. On the basis of their reputation for mystical power and piety, they draw disciples into the *pir-murid* relationship. The *pir* offers spiritual advice and blessing in return for complete obedience. Here as elsewhere is the basis for a *pir's* political influence. Another basis is landowner-ship—land acquired as gifts to their ancestors' shrines. Significantly *pirs* were the only non-Pathans traditionally allowed to own land. Although this did not entitle them to sit in *jirgas*, it did enable them to build independent power bases, from which they could compete for political dominance.

The traditional mediatory role of *Pirs*, moreover, took on a special significance in Frontier society and added to their power to influence. The *Pirs* not only mediated between God and man, but between man and man. This latter role was particularly important in a society divided by mistrust and lineage rivalries. The fact that many *Pirs* were non-Pathans increased their status and standing as impartial brokers amongst quarrelling and contending kinsmen.

Pirs continued to play important roles as alternative sources of political leadership to the tribal elite in Pathan society during the colonial period. Important *Pir* families involved in politics included the Pir Khels of Kohat, Jadun Pirs of Rajuya, Kaka Khel Mians, Gilani Pirs of Kohat, and the Manki Pirs. The Pir of Manki was to play a particularly prominent role in spreading the Muslim League's message to the Frontier.

(e) *The Historical Background.* Politics in the Frontier during the 1940s were profoundly affected by four earlier historical developments, namely the British system of in-direct rule, the impact of the Khilafat Movement, the Reforms Issue, and the legacy of the period of Civil Disobedience in 1930-2. It is necessary, therefore, to briefly examine these earlier influences.

The British turned to the leading Khans to maintain their authority. In return for Government patronage,[8] the Khans used their traditional power to keep the peace and ensure the collection of land revenue. This system worked well until the 1920s when growing tenant discontent and rivalries within the Khanite class put it in jeopardy. The challenges to the British system of indirect rule had their roots both in the worldwide agricultural slump which exacerbated class tensions particularly in the more commercially advanced Peshawar valley, and in the abandonment of their traditional sources of power by many large Khans who came to increasingly rely on British backing for their authority. Small Khans who belonged to the cadet branches of Khan families seized the opportunity to overthrow their traditional rivals. Significantly, the leadership of the Congress–*Khudai Khidmatgar Movement* was provided by young men from the smaller Khan families,[9] whilst its rank and file came from tenants and artisans and client groups. The pro-government larger Khans were thus drawn into opposition of this Movement and many later turned to the Muslim League to safeguard their interests.[10] *'Parajamba'* thus played an important role in structuring nationalist politics in the Frontier, British officials themselves came to recognize that their over-reliance on the large Khans had created the conditions for the growth of the Congress movement, by both antagonizing the rival smaller Khans and by blocking tenants' aspirations for economic and social reform.[11]

The movement in 1919 of Indian Muslims against the harsh peace terms of the Treaty of Sevres imposed on the Turkish Sultan–the Khalifa of Islam–had a lasting impact on Frontier politics. The region's close proximity to Afghanistan, the goal of most of *muhajirs* (exiles) in the ill-fated *'Hijrat'* movement launched by the Khilafat campaign meant that it was greatly affected by it. The Congress's support for the Khilafatists created a tradition of co-operation between Frontier Muslims and this All-India, mainly Hindu, organization. Most importantly, the core of the later more broadly-based Congress *Khudai Khidmatgar Movement* lay in those Muslims who supported the Khilafat campaign and rose to prominence during it. Most notably, of course, the Khan brothers, Abdul Ghaffar Khan and Dr. Khan Sahib, who for a generation were the outstanding political leaders of the Frontier Province. The link between the Khilafat Movement and the *Khudai Khidmatgar Movement* ran directly through such organizations as the *Anjuman-i-Islah-ul-Afghania* (Society for the Reform of the Afghans) which was formed in the wake of the collapse of the *'Hijrat'* movement.

The Reforms controversy strengthened the anti-British and pro-Congress attitudes which had emerged during the Khilafat Movement amongst the younger section of the Khanite elite. Security considerations had made the British wary of introducing political reforms which might endanger the Frontier's stability. The Province was thus excluded from the constitutional rights granted by the *Morley-Minto* and *Montagu-Chelmsford Reforms*. This not only alienated the tiny educated urban elite, but many of the smaller Khans who did not receive the Government's patronage. Both, the Muslim League, and more importantly, the Indian National Congress from 1927 onwards maintained that Reforms should be extended to the North-West Frontier Province. Anti-British attitudes were further engendered in 1924 by events in neighbouring Afghanistan where the uprising of a Tajik outlaw Bacha-i-Saqao was seen as a British attempt to destabilize the country. This was the background to Abdul Ghaffar Khan's formation of the *Afghan Jirga*[12] in 1929. It called for social and economic reform at the expense of the pro-British larger Khans, and promised to work with the Congress for the achievement of Independence. The movement quickly established a strong party organization in the Peshawar valley, basing its support around the factions of the smaller Khans. It was weakest in the Hazara district where its Pathan cultural appeal carried little weight and where the Khattak landlords remained loyal to the British.

The alliance between the *Afghan Jirga* and the Congress which eventually resulted in their merger was cemented by the 1930 Civil Disobedience campaign in Peshawar. This campaign, which began with the riots of 23 April, created the martyrs and myths of the *Khudai Khidmatgar Movement* which were to sustain it until the eve of Independence. The riots increased anti-British feeling and led to uprisings in the Tribal Areas, they also led to the rapid expansion of the quasi-military *Khudai Khidmatgar* volunteer movement which eclipsed its parent body, the *Afghan Jirga*. Most importantly, the Provincial Congress Committee was merged with the *Afghan Jirga* and thereafter was in the pocket of the Khan brothers. In return for allowing this, the All-India Working Committee was henceforth able to claim that it had a bastion of support in a leading Muslim majority province. In reality, however, the Frontier Congress was very much the creation of unique historical circumstances. Despite Abdul Ghaffar Khan's close links with Gandhi and his support for the All-India Civil Disobedience campaigns of the 1930s, the main concern of the Frontier Congress was with parochial Pathan interests, whilst its organization depended on the factions which made up traditional Pathan politics. Its leaders intentionally used the *Khudai Khidmatgar*[13] label instead of the Congress one and even called Congress committees civil *jirgas*. In a real sense despite their paper unity the Congress and the *Khudai Khidmatgar Movement* were separate organizations. Congress influence only existed in the region because of the link with the former 'independent' provincial movement. All-India Congress leaders had to allow this state of affairs to exist in order to maintain the claim that they had the support of a Muslim region.[14]

THE MUSLIM LEAGUE AND FRONTIER POLITICS, 1937-9

The Muslim League possessed little influence in Frontier politics during the years 1937-9. It laboured under the handicap of being unable to secure support in the politically crucial rural Pathan regions. It was a Party of urban lawyers and non-Pathan Muslims residing in the Hazara region, in other words, those on the margins of Frontier society. Nevertheless, the conditions were being created in these years for it to win the backing of the large Khans and thus secure a foothold in power. A Frontier Muslim League had been formed as early as 1912. Its organizers were drawn from the educated population of Peshawar who were preoccupied with pan-Islamic issues. Government repression at the beginning of the First World War brought a permanent halt to this early attempt at organization.[15] The next attempt to form a Frontier League occurred in 1934. This too was unsuccessful. Jinnah thus faced a highly unpromising situation when he journeyed to the Frontier in October 1936 to form a Parliamentary Board in order to fight the first elections to be held under the terms of the Government of India Act, 1935. The weakness of the Muslim League's position was starkly revealed in the composition of the eighteen-man Parliamentary Board. This contained urban, mainly Peshawari, politicians who had been associated with such moribund parties as the Peshawar Khilafat Committee and the Azad Party. Six members of the Board promptly deserted it for the Congress, thus sounding its death knell. Its two members who actually were elected, P.R. Bakhsh and Malik Khuda Bakhsh, stood as Azad Party members rather than Muslim Leaguers.

The Congress, in stark contrast, organized a series of successful mass meetings even though Abdul Ghaffar Khan was still banned from the Province. The limited franchise[16] and strength of traditional rivalries ensured, however, that outside of the Congress's Peshawar valley stronghold, personal loyalties and factional considerations rather than party issues and organization would determine the outcome. The Congress adapted itself to this circumstance by fielding candidates of 'influence'. This was not always possible, however, because it had alienated many of the larger Khans. A large number of these were returned as independent candidates, particularly in the Kohat, Bannu, and Dera Ismail Khan districts. The Congress was also unsuccessful in the Hindu and Sikh constituencies where it lost three of the seven seats it contested to the Hindu-Sikh Nationalist Party.[17] Despite its pre-election hopes, therefore, the Congress did not win a clear majority. The balance of power lay with the Hindu-Sikh Nationalists and the bloc of independent Khans. A number of the latter were organized by the former Minister for Transferred Subjects,[18] named Sir Sahibzada Abdul Qaiyum, into what was called the United Muslim Nationalist Party. Members of this Party formed the future nucleus of the Frontier Muslim League. They turned to the League not because they sympathized with its All-India ideals, but because it offered them protection. This was necessary after the attacks on their interests launched by the brief Frontier Congress regime of Dr. Khan Sahib. Before turning to the measures of this Congress government, however, it is first important to examine the Qaiyum coalition which preceded it.

The Congress Working Committee's hesitation over office acceptance enabled the Frontier Governor, Sir George Cunningham, to engineer a non-Congress coalition government headed by Sir Abdul Qaiyum. This coalition was so inherently unstable that it only survived five months before the Congress replaced it. The United Muslim Nationalist Party disintegrated upon the government's collapse. It was the Muslim League, however, rather than the Congress which was chief beneficiary. Whilst still in office, Sir Abdul Qaiyum discreetly encouraged the formation of a Frontier Muslim League organization as a counterweight to the Congress. This was headed in September 1937 by Maulana Muhammad Shuaib. The real breakthrough for the League came, however, when a number of influential Khans who were Sir Abdul Qaiyum's allies formed a Peshawar District Muslim League on 23 October 1937. At a compromise meeting held in Nowshera on 3 November 1937, both the District League and the Provincial League were disbanded and a new League Council emerged.[19] Its strength was still greatest in non-Pathan areas where there was considerable opposition to the stress which the *Khudai Khidmatgars* placed on Pathan culture and the Pushtu language.[20] The League had also, however, gained the support of a number of the large Khans. In order to understand their new-found allegiance, we need to turn to the period of the Khan Sahib ministry of September 1937 to November 1939.

The Congress organization revived quickly during the time of the Khan Sahib ministry. Years of government repression were replaced with a favourable environment for the expansion of its influence. By 1939, Congress and *Khudai Khidmatgar* membership stood at around 80,000. Even more worrying for the large Khans, however, was the attack on their influence launched by the government. Their pivotal position in local administration was removed with the abolition of the Honorary Magistrate and *Zaildar* system; their rights to revenue remission in return for services to government were ended; they were discriminated against when it came to the distribution of arms licences and in the allocation of agricultural improvement loans. Finally and most dangerously of all, the government encouraged tenants in their refusal to pay rent to their landlords. When it became clear that the British would not intervene to safeguard the large Khans' interests, many of them turned to the Muslim League for protection. The decline in Congress membership which followed on from the decision of the Khan Sahib ministry to resign in 1939 in protest at the Viceroy's declaring war on India's behalf further boosted the League's fortunes. It was not, however, until 1943 with many of the Congress MLAs locked up, that the Frontier League was able to take sufficient advantage of the situation to form a ministry.[21] Aurangzeb Khan's period in office, however, resulted not in a consolidation of the Muslim League's influence in the Frontier, but rather initiated a crisis which afflicted the Party down to the vital 1946 Provincial Elections.

THE LEAGUE IN POWER

During its two year period in office, the Aurangzeb Khan ministry became notorious for its corruption. It also lost much Muslim support in the way it handled commodity scarcities and rising prices. Most damagingly of all it came into conflict with its own party organization. By June 1944, the situation had become so catastrophic that the All-India Muslim League Council had to order its Committee of Action to conduct a full-scale investigation into the Frontier League. The subsequent reorganization had barely got underway when Dr. Khan Sahib brought down the ministry bringing to a close a sordid and unhappy episode in the Frontier League's history.

Many of the Aurangzeb Khan ministry's problems could be traced to its inception in May 1943. Although Jinnah claimed that the ministry's formation showed the growth of support for the League in the Frontier, in reality Aurangzeb Khan's position from the outset was shaky. He would never have come to power if ten of the Congress members had not been in jail. Even so, he had to scrape the barrel in order to achieve the twenty-two Assembly votes necessary to form a government. He won the support of a number of independent Khans, not because they had been converted to the League's ideas, but rather because he held out to them the prospect of rich government pickings. Herein lay the seeds of the growing corruption which eventually alienated even the Muslim League's own supporters.

Corruption had traditionally oiled the wheels of Frontier politics, but it had never been as blatant as during Aurangzeb's ministry. In order to stay in power, he had to placate the large Khans who were eager to recoup the losses they had sustained during the Congress period of rule. 'The

whole Khanite class flocked into the Muslim League like
vultures over a corpse', a local League worker wrote despair-
ingly to Jinnah, 'The ministers got salaries and bribes, and
members of the League Party got permits [whilst] the masses
groaned under war conditions'.[22] The pro-League *Khyber
Mail* similarly protested: 'Corruption with a capital C is writ
large on the face of the Frontier administration and almost
everybody who has anything to do with the administrative
machinery there bothers about just one thing—how best to
feather his own nest'.[23]

The greatest criticism was reserved for corruption in the
management of wartime rationing. According to one Muslim
Leaguer, the ministry 'had dragged the name of the Frontier
League in the dust' in the way it handled 'contracts, permits
and membership of syndicates for the distribution of wheat'.[24]
It is undoubtedly true that the ministers used the allocation
of scarce resources to pay off political supporters. The
government also less fairly had to face up to the unpopularity
caused by the need for the requisitioning of food grains, and
the mandatory specification of crop acreage. Both policies
were necessary to prevent famine in the deficit areas of the
province; nevertheless, they alienated the *zamindars*. In a
supreme irony, whilst the Muslim League in neighbouring
Punjab was making use of rural discontent with requisitioning to undermine the Unionist government, in the Frontier
its government was losing popularity precisely because it
was following those same measures.

The Aurangzeb Khan ministry's problems were
compounded by the mounting hostility it faced from the
organizational wing of the Frontier League. Clashes between
Muslim League ministers and provincial officials were by no
means confined to the Frontier. Similar rivalry occurred in
both Sind and Bengal. It was partly rooted in personal
rivalries and the inevitable resentment the 'outs' felt towards
the political 'ins'. Ideological considerations also played
a part. Ministers' compromises and use of patronage

frequently alienated League workers who possessed a loftier conception of the League's cause. The clash between them took on a particularly serious character in the Frontier because of the personal enmity between the Chief Minister, Aurangzeb Khan, and the former League President Saadullah Khan. It totally undermined the League's poor organizational development in the region.

Saadullah Khan began intriguing against the Premier within weeks of the ministry's formation. Their rivalry in fact went back several years. It had taken on the form of a vendetta after Aurangzeb Khan had arranged for criminal proceedings to be brought against his rival and had subjected him to the dishonour of having his house searched for allegedly hoarding unlicensed weapons.[25] Matters came to a head at the Council League meeting held on 25 March 1945, its proceedings degenerated into a shouting match between their two sets of supporters. 'There was no discipline and no respect for the Chair', a local journalist, Abdur Rahman, reported. 'Most of the Khans participating in the meeting were armed to the teeth.'[26] Even before this fiasco, however, the All-India leadership had instituted an enquiry into the Frontier League's affairs.

The Committee of Action of the All-India Muslim League Council toured the Frontier between 13 to 29 June 1944. Its report made depressing reading for Jinnah. It detailed the deterioration in the League's work, arising from the lack of co-operation between ministers and local officials. It also revealed the rampant corruption and shortages of rationed commodities, which had led League officials to call for resignation of the ministers before further damage was done to their organization's reputation.[27] Equally worrying was the Provincial League Secretary's own admission that 'on paper there are District Leagues in every district, but from some districts, I have never received any replies to communications. The 2-anna membership doesn't exist any-where in the Province as far as I know'.[28] The Committee of

Action's report concluded that there was 'no organization worth the name in the Province'.[29] Thus, it recommended that the Frontier League be suspended. One of its members, Qazi Isa, a Pathan from Baluchistan, was entrusted with the arduous job of overhauling the League organization. Qazi Isa commenced this task on 9 October 1944. He toured the Frontier in order to re-establish Primary branches of the League. Little progress had been made, however, by the time of the resignation of the Muslim League ministry on 14 March 1945. The release of Congress legislators as the war drew to a close made the government's defeat increasingly likely. Nevertheless, it was worrying for League officials that a motion of no-confidence had been eventually lost because of defection of Saadullah Khan and four of his supporters. The reorganization of the Frontier League had led, in fact, to increased factionalism rather than growing unity. The anti-ministerialist forces and the supporters of Aurangzeb Khan each contended for control of the *ad hoc* committees established by Qazi Isa to run the League organization. Local workers made a series of bitter complaints to the All-India leadership when it became clear that members of Aurangzeb Khan's faction were acquiring a dominant position on the committees. One writer asserted that Qazi Isa was misleading Jinnah about the strength of the League in the Frontier and had hardly stirred from the luxury of Deans Hotel in Peshawar when he was supposed to be organizing the League.[30] Another suggested that the Frontier League should be given over to the control of the Punjab League and 'enthusiastic workers like Shaukat Hayat and Maulana Zafar Ali Khan'.[31] The charge was also made that members of the *ad hoc* committees discouraged genuine League workers 'whose only interest was to make the Muslim League strong for the attainment of Pakistan' because they saw the death of their vested interests in 'such mass work'.[32] The opposition to Aurangzeb Khan and his followers was so deep-seated in Peshawar city that a rival 'Progressive Muslim League' was formed. It was, therefore, with considerable relief that the Central League authorities were able to postpone further reorganization in the summer of 1945, in order to concentrate energies on the forthcoming provincial elections.

THE 1946 ELECTIONS

The Frontier Muslim League approached the 1946 Provincial Elections poorly organized and internally divided. There was little if any co-ordination between the activities of the Finance Board and the Election Board set up to manage the campaign.[33] In Peshawar, local workers were so incensed by the choice of candidate of the Selection Board that they ceased working for the League.[34] Elsewhere in the province there was also disquiet at the number of tickets given to partisans of Aurangzeb Khan: Asadul Haq from Abbottabad complained that this showed absolute disregard for elementary principles of justice and fair play. 'People ask, is this the type of Pakistan that is to come?' he lamented to Jinnah, 'and we in shame have no answer to give'.[35] Such dissension contrasted badly with the unanimity of the Congress's selective procedure.

Ardent supporters of the League, however, believed that enthusiasm for the Pakistan demand would ensure victory, despite the weaknesses in organization. Jinnah, in a tour of the Frontier in late November 1945, had starkly warned that: 'Every vote in favour of the Muslim League candidates means Pakistan. Every vote against the Muslim League candidates means Hindu Raj'.[36] This message was amplified by student workers from the Punjab and Aligarh. Unfortunately, for the Muslim League, it meant little to the mass of rural Pathan voters.[37] They did not fear Hindu domination. Nor were they convinced that the *Khudai Khidmatgars* were anti-Muslim and tools of the Hindus. The Congress anti-British propaganda, and its attacks on the large Khans were, in fact, far more effective. It was not, however, party programmes and organization which in any case ultimately decided the outcome. Traditional factional rivalries and treating of the voters were far more important. This point was recognized by the Governor when he wrote to the Viceroy, shortly before polling began on 26 January. 'In Bannu district, where I spent three days recently, the results in the voting for the Muslim seats seem likely to be decided by the number of sheep each candidate can kill to feast his supporters. One was said to have killed 93 sheep already and the general estimate is 10 votes per sheep'.[38]

The Muslim League appeared well prepared for an election fought on the grounds of personal factional feeling rather than grand political issues. It included amongst its candidates many of the leading Khans of the Province, such men as Nawab Sir Muhammed Akbar Khan, the Khan of Hoti,[39] Nawab Mohabbat Ali Khan, the Khan of Kohat, Nawab Qutbuddin Khan, the descendant of the pre-British rulers of Tank, and a major jagirdar, Mir Alam Khan, one of the largest landlords in the Peshawar valley, and Muhammed Zaman Khan, the Khan of Khalubat, to name but a few. The League also had the support of a number of important Pir families. The Pir of Zakeri was the successful League candidate in the Lakki West constituency in Dera Ismail Khan. The Pir of Manki ordered his murids in the Koh-i-Daman area to support the Muslim League candidate for Buta Mohmands.[40] He also formed an organization known as the Anjuman-us-Asfia to co-ordinate the activities of the province's pirs on the Muslim League's behalf.

Beneath the surface, however, all was not well with the League's attempt to use gundi and piri-mureedi ties to mobilize support. The Congress also had men of influence standing as its candidates. There was, for example, Pir Shahinshah of Jangal Khel, and Muhammad Yakub Khan and Akbar Ali Khan, two leading Maliks of the Bannuchi Tribe of the Bannu district. More importantly those members of the traditional rural elite who supported the Congress were disciplined and loyal to its organization. This was not the case with the Muslim League. The Khan of Kohat lost in the Kohat constituency mainly because *Pir* Syed Jalal refused to support him after he had been passed over for the Muslim League ticket. Similarly, in the Nowshera constituency leading pro-League Khattak Khans refused to support the League candidate after being denied a League ticket. Such disunity exacerbated the major weakness in the League's electoral strategy. This was the fact that many of the large Khans on whom it relied had lost their traditional authority and influence. Their place had been taken by younger men drawn from the junior branches of Khan families. They were well represented in the Congress, but had been ignored by the Muslim League. In many constituencies in the Peshawar and Mardan districts, pro-League senior Khans were defeated by Congress candidates of such junior status. Arbab Abdur Rahman Khan of the junior branch of the Dandazi Arbabs defeated the head of the Dandazi Tribe in the Doaba-Dandazi constituency. Abdul Aziz Khan, a member of a junior branch of the Zaida Khans, won for the Congress at Utmannama in Mardan, Muhammad Aslam Khan similarly succeeded from a modest status at Teri North in Kohat. Significantly, the Muslim League recorded its best results in Hazara district where the large landholders still exerted an iron grip over the countryside.[41]

When the votes were counted early in February 1946, it soon became clear that the Muslim League had suffered a major setback in the Frontier. The Congress had clearly emerged as the major party, capturing 30 of the 50 seats. Its allies in the *Jamiat-ulema-i-Hind* had won two more, and it could also rely on the vote of the one Parthic Sikh member. Most damaging for the Muslim League, however, was the fact that the Congress had secured 19 of the 36 seats reserved for Muslims. These included the bulk of the rural Pathan constituencies. The Muslim League still remained the party of the towns and of the non-Pathan Hazara district. Yet, just over a year later, the Pathans along with the province's other Muslims, voted overwhelmingly for the inclusion of the Frontier in Pakistan. What lay behind this dramatic transformation in the Muslim League's fortunes?

THE TRIUMPH OF THE MUSLIM LEAGUE

The changing political situation elsewhere in India, the deteriorating communal situation in the Frontier itself, and the reorganization of the Muslim League all played important roles in the triumphant Referendum Campaign of June 1947. Before examining these factors it is first necessary, however, to analyze the 1946 election results in further detail.

It should be noted that the elections, unlike the later Referendum, were concerned with local issues, rather than the question of Pakistan itself, despite the Muslim League propaganda to that effect. Moreover, Pathan support for the Frontier Congress did not mean wholehearted agreement with its parent body's All-India aims and interests. This point was perceptively picked up by Governor Cunningham. He saw that the Congress's victory owed much to the fact that 'the Pathan simply cannot conceive of a situation in which his comings and goings would really be regulated by an outside non-Muslim authority'. He thus warned the Viceroy that 'It would be dangerous ... to assume from the present set-up that the Pathan as such will be quite happy in a unified India without safeguards for himself'.[42] The fact that the Congress's real strength in the Province was weaker than its overwhelming predominance in the Legislative Assembly also had an important bearing on subsequent developments. Nearly a quarter of the seats, all but one of which the Congress had captured, were reserved for the minority Hindu and Sikh communities which together accounted for less than 10 per cent of the population. Here then was a considerable weightage in the Congress's favour. When it came to the 36 Muslim seats, moreover, the Congress's performance in terms of the percentage of the votes cast was less impressive than its haul of seats. In its heartland of the 22 rural Pathan constituencies, the Congress captured 51 per cent of the total votes, while the Muslim League polled 39 per cent. In the Muslim rural constituencies as a whole, however, the Muslim League did considerably better, winning 40.7 per cent to the Congress's 41.1 per cent, whilst in the towns it came into its own garnering 43.6 per cent of the votes, with the Congress trailing with 22.2 per cent. This meant that overall, the Muslim League won a slightly larger percentage (41-39 per cent) of the rural Muslim votes cast, although it secured two fewer seats than the Congress.[43] Although Dr. Khan Sahib was able to once more form a Congress government following the 1946 elections, the Frontier League had a firm base on which to build. Events outside the region soon assisted its rise to power.

Frontier politics previously revolved around local interests and issues (as they had done elsewhere in India) during the period of Dyarchy and Provincial Autonomy. The region was affected by political developments at the centre which could shape the framework of local politics, but down to 1945 such external impulses remained of secondary importance; parochial interests and concerns predominated. At the end of the war, however, provincial politicians throughout India were faced with the need to adjust their position in the light of the rapidly changing situation at the centre.[44] Large numbers of Muslim politicians in Punjab and Bengal linked their fortunes with the ascendant star of the Muslim League following the July 1945 Simla Conference. The converts to the League were far fewer[45] in the Frontier because its relative remoteness and weak non-Muslim minority at first lessened the impact of the communalization of Indian politics. Within a few months of the 1946 elections, however, events outside the Frontier were exerting a major influence on the course of its provincial politics.

The *Cabinet Mission* proposals of May 1946 dealt the first major blow to the Frontier Congress's position. Its leaders had always been vague about the future of the Frontier region. They now faced an unenviable choice of options, grouping with Sind and Punjab and thus being swamped by their Muslim League opponents, or joining with Madras, Bombay, Central Provinces, Bihar, Orissa, and the United Provinces with its massive Hindu majority. The Muslim League's claims that the choice facing the Frontier Muslims was either *Akhand* (undivided) Hindustan or Pakistan over-night took on a reality that had been missing during the earlier provincial elections. The collapse of the *Cabinet Mission Scheme* did not make this reality any less uncomfortable for the Congress leaders. Indeed, Nehru's ill-judged visit to the Tribal Areas the following October brought it home even more clearly to the Pathans that they might one day be ruled by a Hindu-dominated centre.[46]

The Frontier Congress blamed the British for instigating the hostile demonstrations against Nehru.[47] In reality, it resulted from the Tribesmen's response to news of communal violence elsewhere in India. There was a similar reaction in the Frontier Province itself, causing immense damage to the Congress's reputation. Like its counterpart in Sind, the Frontier League made great propaganda out of the communal disorders in Bombay, Noakhali, and Bihar which followed in the wake of the Great Calcutta Killing of 16 August. The medical missions which it sent to Bihar not only provided humanitarian assistance to the Muslim victims of the riots, but served the useful purpose of providing vivid first-hand accounts of the destruction. Workers returned brandishing blood-stained clothing and even the skulls of alleged Muslim victims.[48] The press published lurid reports of the Hindu atrocities on innocent men, women, and children. The fact that a large number of migrant Pathan workers lived in Bombay, some of whom were caught up in the September Hindu-Muslim riots, increased their impact on the Frontier. Muslim Congressmen faced an increasingly difficult situation as reports filtered through of horrible carnage. The Muslim League demanded that they should show solidarity with their suffering Muslim brothers elsewhere by joining its ranks. The strong sense of Islamic *asbiyyat* community, indeed, led many to desert the Congress at this time.

The Muslim League not only gained from communal troubles, elsewhere in India, but also from increasing religious antagonisms within the Frontier itself. Violence flared up in December 1946, when trans-border Tribesmen began raiding in the Hazara district. Hindu and Sikh businesses were destroyed and there was a large exodus of the religious minorities to the neighbouring Rawalpindi district of the Punjab.[49] Before order could be fully restored, communal disturbances began elsewhere in the Province in the wake of the Muslim League campaign of Civil Disobedience against the Khan Sahib ministry.

The Frontier League began its campaign shortly after a similar movement had been launched against the Unionist ministry in the Punjab. In both instances, direct action was a premeditated attempt to demonstrate the Muslim League's command over the loyalty of the Muslim population at a time when Partition was becoming increasingly likely. Frustration at exclusion from power by what were regarded as unrepresentative governments fuelled both movements. They were essentially local campaigns, directed by the provincial Leagues and launched on their decision rather than that of the All-India League leaders. The arrest of many front rank local leaders increased the decentralization of the campaigns. They were genuinely popular movements involving not only local officials and party organizers, but ordinary people as well. Women[50] and students played a prominent role in the campaigns which severely disrupted the administration of both Punjab and the Frontier. Direct action demonstrated more effectively than legislative politics the growing hold which the Muslim League exerted on the life of these north-western regions of India. There was, however, also a dark side to civil disobedience. This was mounting communal tensions. In the Punjab, it broke out in the wake of the Unionist ministry's resignation on 4 March, in the Frontier—with police firing on a Muslim League procession in Peshawar on 10 March. The breakdown of government control in both provinces left the isolated Hindu and Sikh communities of the north-western regions at the mercy of angry Muslim mobs.[51]

During March 1947, civil disorder and its accompanying communal violence was centred in Hazara and Peshawar. The government responded by arresting the *Pir* of Manki who had played a major role in organizing the League campaign. It also sent thousands of *Khudai Khidmatgars* into Peshawar city to help restore order, much to the dismay of British officials.[52] The Governor, Caroe, viewed with alarm the increase in size of para-military groups.[53] Although armed clashes between them were prevented, serious disturbances spread to the Dera Ismail Khan region early in April. The number of casualties were not high, in comparison with the later carnage in the Punjab, but the damage to Hindu and Sikh property was unprecedented. One crore rupees worth of damage was estimated to have occurred in Dera Ismail Khan, where about 900 shops were destroyed by fire,[54] whilst neighbouring Tank was almost burnt to the ground. The havoc was wreaked partly by mobs of Muslim League supporters, and partly by Mahsuds raiding from the tribal territories. Thousands of Hindus and Sikhs fled from the region.

The use of communal violence to achieve political ends was not confined to the Frontier Muslim League organization, nor to the Muslim community, as British rule drew to its close. The Frontier League secured its objective, when the new Viceroy, Lord Mountbatten, made it clear that he would insist on fresh elections or a referendum before deciding on the region's future. It was easier, however, to arouse communal disturbances than to halt them. They continued in the Frontier even after the League had secured its objective and Jinnah had personally issued an appeal that the violence should cease.[55]

The communal disorders overshadowed the reorganization of the Provincial League organization which went on throughout the second half of 1946. Part of the process of giving new impetus to the Frontier Muslim League involved the convening of a series of Pakistan Conferences. The *Pir* of Manki organized and addressed a spate of such meetings in the Peshawar and Mardan districts early in September 1946.[56] These succeeded earlier successful conferences in Peshawar in April. During these, *Pir* Jamiat Ali Shah of Alipur in Punjab had attacked Congress Muslims as being anti-Islamic in sentiment and practices.[57] In November, political meetings were organized in Dera Ismail Khan and Tank. These were again addressed by *Pir* of Manki and many tribesmen from the neighbouring Agency[58] attended them.

The Frontier League organization was also given an overhaul. Qazi Isa's *ad hoc* committees were replaced by a new forty-three member Provincial Muslim League Organizing Committee which was instructed by the All-India Muslim League's Committee of Action to enroll new party members, conduct party elections, and establish a local League organization. The deteriorating communal situation throughout India had led to an almost daily exodus of members from the Frontier Congress. Some of the most prominent recent converts to the League were included in its new provincial party leadership. These included such men as Ghulam Mohammad Khan, a former president of the Frontier Congress, and Arbab Abdul Ghaffar, one of the *Afghan Jirga's* main organizers in Peshawar. Even the Organizing Committee's Chairman, Khan Mohammad Samin Khan, was a former Congressman. Three of its members had, in fact, defeated Muslim League candidates in the 1946 Provincial Elections.[59] Long-standing members of the League were scandalized by the entry of a few 'turn-coats' into positions of authority.[60] The Frontier League needed such recent converts, however, because they brought not only desperately needed organizational skills, but also the support of their large faction-followings. When the head of the Kandi Tribe of Dera Ismail Khan defected from the Congress, the Muslim League was reckoned to have gained some 6,000 votes.[61] Like its counterparts in Punjab and Bengal, the Frontier League could not afford to rebuff offers of support from such men of influence, despite the newness of their conversion to its cause. Everything had to be subordinated to achieving Pakistan, it - would be for the Government of Pakistan to discipline and weed out opportunists from the Muslim League's ranks.

INDIA, PAKISTAN OR *PAKHTUNISTAN?*

The Muslim League's unceasing campaign of disruption early in 1947 almost stretched British resources to breaking point. The Governor, Sir Olaf Caroe,[62] became convinced that the continuation of the Congress ministry was a major threat to peace not only in the province but in the surrounding turbulent Tribal Areas. He, therefore, pressed for the holding of fresh elections. When Mountbatten raised this idea to Nehru, however, the latter strongly protested. Mountbatten journeyed to Peshawar on 28 to 29 April 1947 to see the situation for himself. The Muslim League seized the opportunity to demonstrate its power, by gathering a vast crowd nearly 100,000 strong which was only prevented from storming the Government House by Mountbatten's agreeing to show his face to it. He later gave an interview to a Muslim League delegation, six of whom were on parole from jail. The following day at Landi Kotal he met leaders of the Mahsuds and Wazirs who expressed strong support for the Pakistan demand and condemned the Congress Government.

When Mountbatten returned to New Delhi, he decided that although fresh elections were not practical, a referendum must be held before the Frontier's future was decided. Both the Secretary of State[63] and Nehru still expressed misgivings. The former because it might set an awkward precedent for

Punjab and Bengal, the latter, because holding a plebiscite would be yielding to force.[64] The Viceroy overruled these objections, pointing out that Caroe foresaw 'a real flare-up in the province' unless an election or referendum were held.[65]

The Frontier Congress leaders were naturally bitterly opposed to the idea of a plebiscite. From the beginning of May they began to raise their own slogan for an autonomous *Pakhtun* (Pathan) state, *Pakhtunistan*. This demand emerged so late in the day that it was easy for the Muslim League to dismiss it as merely a bargaining counter. For many Frontier Congressmen it was nothing more than that. In a real sense, however, it was the logical conclusion of the Frontier Congress's earlier championing of Pathan interests and culture. It contained within it the powerful sentiment of Pathan fear of Punjabi domination 'in the name of religion'.[66] Although a number of Congress leaders believed that they might even win a plebiscite on the issue of *Pakhtunistan*, this seems unlikely given the communal polarization in India by the summer of 1947. In the event, British security fears about the balkanization of India ensured that the *Pakhtunistan* option was not included in the referendum. Furthermore, it was to take place only after the Punjab and Bengal representatives had voted on the partition of their provinces. With the Punjab's decision for Pakistan a foregone conclusion, support for the Frontier's inclusion in India would have to be given in the knowledge that the region would be physically cut off from the rest of Hindustan. In these circumstances, the Frontier Congressmen saw their defeat pre-ordained. They felt badly let down by the National Congress leadership, and cheated by pro-League British officials. Three weeks before the referendum was due to be held Abdul Ghaffar Khan declared in a public meeting at Bannu that the Congress would boycott it and continue to work peacefully for its *Pakhtunistan* demand.

For the Frontier League on the other hand, the tide of events had turned triumphantly in its favour. Political developments elsewhere in India, together with its own Direct

Action campaign had transformed the political situation. In a few short months, the League had secured a massive swing in public opinion away from the Frontier Congress. Dr. Khan Sahib still remained in office but the League was the real master of the province.

Despite the Congress boycott, the Muslim League left nothing to chance and mounted a vigorous referendum campaign. Its three main organizers were I.I. Chundrigar, the Muslim League Member for Commerce in the Interim Government, the Punjabi League leader, Firoz Khan Noon and Abdul Qaiyum, the leader of the Frontier Muslim League Assembly Party. They sent workers into all the villages popularizing the Pakistan demand.[67] The Congress boycott was denounced as un-Islamic and the religious duty to vote for Pakistan was clearly spelt out.[68] Those Hindus and Sikhs who had returned to the Frontier were warned not to interfere in the voting.[69] Any opposition from the *Khudai Khidmatgars* was prevented by a massive Muslim League show of strength in Peshawar on 20 June. Eight hundred and fifty heavily armed and uniformed National Guards attended the meeting, at which over 2,000 shots were fired in the air.[70]

The total votes cast in the referendum were 292,118 just 2,874 of which were cast for the Frontier's inclusion in India rather than Pakistan.[71] Ninety-nine per cent of the ballots cast were thus in favour of Pakistan. Nevertheless, Pakistan only received 50.49 per cent support from all those eligible to vote. In all, 183,871 fewer votes had been cast than in the 1944 elections. The lower turn-out was, however, only partly the result of the Congress boycott. More important was the fact that the electoral rolls were badly out of date.[72] The most accurate guage of the Muslim League's advance was the fact it had virtually doubled its vote since the time of the provincial elections.

Although Pakistan's creation depended on events elsewhere in the subcontinent, the Muslim League's success in the Frontier Referendum was vital for the viability of the state it desired. For without the Frontier, Pakistan would have led a tenuous existence, even without the Kashmir dispute. The outcome of the Referendum justified the local leadership's resort to direct action, despite the communal disorders it had brought.

The rapid rise in the Muslim League's power in the region during 1946-7, however, created a dangerous illusion of permanence. It had resulted from the sense of *asbiyyat* created by the attacks on the Muslim minorities in Bihar and Bombay. Once the crisis had passed the old factional rivalries and particularism resurfaced. The League lacked the organizational structure to counter these with a programme of nation-building. It soon reverted to its old infighting. Within a year a split had occurred amidst recriminations between Abdul Qaiyum and *Pir* of Manki. The League's influence declined as rapidly as it had grown.

REFERENCE

1. The Frontier region was wrested from the Sikhs by the British in 1849. It was not until 1901, however, that its settled districts were taken out of the Punjab Government's hands and a North-West Frontier Province consisting of Hazara, Peshawar, Kohat, Bannu, and Dera Ismail Khan was formed. In 1937 Peshawar was divided into two and the Mardan District formed.
2. *Census of India*, Vol. XV, Part 1, pp. 40-1.
3. Significantly, the relatively prosperous agricultural region of the Peshawar valley supported 40 per cent of the Province's population. Such barren areas as Kohat were able to support only a sparse population.
4. Three quarters of all Hindus and Sikhs lived in urban areas. Together they accounted for a third of the Frontier's town dwellers.
5. According to their tradition, they entered the region as conquerors in the fifteenth century from their homeland of Ghor in Afghanistan. They owned all land in pre-British times.
6. Herein lies one reason for the Pathan's attitude of superiority, for they have no infidel past, unlike other Muslims, converted from Hinduism.
7. Among some tribes the title is inheritable, as a sign of respect any Pathan landlord can be called a Khan.
8. This took the form of honorary titles, and appointments as magistrates, officials, and subordinate judges.
9. A particularly important role was played by young men of the Muhammed Zai and Mian elite of the Charsadda Tehsil of the Peshawar valley.
10. Stephen Rittenburg's excellent Ph.D., thesis, 'The Independence Movement in India's North-West Frontier Province, 1901-1947', Columbia University, 1977, clearly reveals the intertwining between traditional factional rivalries and the development of the Congress and Muslim League political organizations.

11. Ibid., p. 107.
12. It drew much of its personnel from the *Anjuman-i-Islah-ul-Afghania* and was soon to be overshadowed by its para-military wing, the *Khudai Khidmatgars* (Servants of God), known as the Red Shirts because of their red uniform.
13. Its Islamic overtones was a handicap to Muslim League claims that the Khan brothers had sold out to a Hindu organization.
14. Rittenburg, op. cit., 1977, p. 253.
15. Ibid., p. 57.
16. Just a quarter of a million voters, 14 per cent population.
17. The final results were as follows: Congress 19 seats; Hindu-Sikh Nationalists 7; Azad Party 2; Independents 22.
18. A Legislative Council had been introduced into the Frontier in 1932 in the wake of the Civil Disobedience campaign.
19. This was controlled by the Khans from Peshawar, Maulana Muhammad Shuaib was reduced to a figurehead position. In December 1938 he was finally stripped of his office and replaced by Saadullah Khan. Rittenburg, op. cit., 1977, p. 257.
20. In November 1931 Abdul Ghaffar Khan had outraged audiences in Hazara by denigrating Punjab language and culture and declaring that 'when we have self-government we will have everything in Pushtu'. Rittenburg, op. cit., 1977, p. 176.
21. Aurangzeb Khan, the Provincial League leader, had attempted unsuccessfully to form a ministry in 1939. On his failure, the British had assumed direct control of the Provincial Administration under Section 93 of the *Government of India Act, 1935.*
22. Asadul Haq to Jinnah, 20 December 1945, SHC N.W.F.P., 1:90.
23. *Khyber Mail*, 21 April 1944.
24. Saadullah Khan to Jinnah, 1 September 1945, SHC N.W.F.P., 1:59.
25. Ibid.
26. Abdur Rahman to Liaquat Ali Khan, 28 March 1944, FMA Vol. 344.
27. Proceedings of the visit of the Committee of Action to the North-West Frontier Province, FMA Vol. 343, N.W.F.P., ML Part III, 1944.
28. Statement of Mian Ziauddin, General Secretary, Provincial Muslim League, 22 June 1944.
29. Proceedings of the visit of the Committee of Action to the North-West Frontier Province, FMA Vol. 343, N.W.F.P., ML Part III, 1944.
30. Ghulam Rab Khan to Jinnah, 29 August 1945, SHC N.W.F.P., 1:58.
31. Akhter to Liaquat Ali Khan, 3 April 1945, FMA Vol. 344.
32. Asadul Haq to Jinnah, 20 October 1945, SHC N.W.F.P., 1:90.
33. M. Ziauddin to Liaquat Ali Khan, 2 November 1945, FMA Vol. 344.
34. A. B. Yusufi to Jinnah, 19 December 1945, SHC N.W.F.P., 1:89.
35. Asadul Haq to Jinnah, 20 October 1945, SHC N.W.F.P., 1:90.
36. *Dawn*, 29 November 1945.
37. The British Governor wrote that the Pakistan demand was not really an intelligible war cry to 90 per cent of its hearers, as for the 'average Pathan villager in these parts, the suggestions that there can be such a thing as Hindu domination is only laughable'. Cunningham to Wavell, 27 February 1946, R/3/1/105, IOR.
38. Cunningham to Wavell, 24 January 1946, L/P&J/5/233.
39. Not only a hereditary chief, but the wealthiest landowner in the province.
40. Rittenburg, op. cit., 1977.
41. *Governor's Report*, 27 February 1946, N.W.F.P., FR L/P&J/5/223.
42. Cunningham to Wavell, 23 March 1946, R/3/105 IOR.
43. Computed from Dhawan, A.S., *Report on the General Elections to the Central Assembly and to the NWFP Legislative Assembly*, Peshawar, 1946.
44. Notably the imminent departure of the British and the jockeying for power at the Centre between the All-India National Congress and the All-India Muslim League.

45. The most notable convert was Abdul Qaiyum, former Congress Deputy Leader in the Central Assembly. He was joined by Arbab Abdul Ghaffar and a few other *Afghan Jirga* Congress dissidents.

46. Nehru had made the visit against the advice of both British officials and some of the members of the Congress High Command. It provided the Muslim League with an ideal symbol of future Hindu domination. After receiving a hostile welcome in Peshawar, Nehru seriously put his life at risk in a series of discussion trips to the Tribal Areas. Wavell to Pethick Lawrence, 22 October 1946, L/P&J/5/223 IOR.

47. Ibid.

48. *Tribune*, 10 January 1947; N.W.F.P., FR, second half of January 1947, L/P&J/5/224 IOR.

49. N.W.F.P., FR, first half of January 1947, L/P&J/5/224 IOR.

50. *Purdah* women took out daily demonstrations in Peshawar, they stormed into the Secretariat and distributed free 'Pakistan tickets' at railway offices. Rittenburg, op. cit., 1977, p. 376 and ff.

51. The Sikh campaign of terror in Central and Eastern Punjab in the summer of 1947 was prompted by the desire to revenge the earlier Muslim attacks in the Frontier and north-west Punjab.

52. N.W.F.P., FR, second half of March 1947, L/P&J/5/244 IOR.

53. The Red Shirts numbered 8,000 at the beginning of 1947. There were some 5,000 Muslim League National Guards, and 2,000 members of the Hindu RSSS N.W.F.P., second half of January 1947, L/P&J/5/244 IOR.

54. N.W.F.P., FR, second half of April 1947, L/P&J/5/224 IOR.

55. Rittenburg, op. cit., 1977, p. 375.

56. Caroe to Wavell, N.W.F.P., FR, first half of September 1946, L/P&J/5/223 IOR.

57. N.W.F.P., FR, second half of April 1946, L/P&J/5/223 IOR.

58. N.W.F.P., FR, first half of November 1946, L/P&J/5/223 IOR.

59. Mian Ziauddin to Nawab Ismail Khan, 6 June 1946, FMA Vol. 366, N.W.F.P., Provincial Muslim League 1946-7.

60. Ibid.

61. Caroe to Wavell, Telegram of 25 June 1947, R/3/1/151 IOR.

62. Caroe's career as Governor evoked great controversy. Khan Abdul Ghaffar Khan believed he was biased in favour of the Muslim League and demanded his replacement. The incessant allegations against him eventually led Mountbatten to engineer his temporary leave of absence from 6 June until after the date of the Transfer of Power.

63. Secretary of State to Mountbatten, 6 May 1947, R/3/1/151.

64. Mountbatten to Secretary of State, 8 May 1947.

65. Ibid.

66. *Tribune*, 15 May 1947.

67. Governor to Viceroy, 17 June 1947, R/3/1/151 IOR.

68. The choice was between idol worship in temples, or prayer in mosques as ordered in the Holy Qur'an by the Holy Prophet. *Tribune*, 27 June 1947.

69. Governor to Viceroy, 17 June 1947, R/3/1/151 IOR.

70. Governor to Viceroy, 21 June 1947, R/3/1/151 IOR.

71. Referendum Commissioner, 19 July 1947, R/3/1/151 IOR.

72. They had not been revised since 1945.

2
The Struggles within Sind

After the Punjab, Sind was the most important province in the bloc of Muslim majority provinces in north-western India in terms of both population and economic strength.[1] The region was thus of considerable importance for the Muslim League's separatist demands. Indeed, it had a close symbolic relationship with the very idea of Pakistan. For its separation from Bombay Presidency in 1936 in a sense foreshadowed the larger Partition of India a decade later. Although it did not face an organized opposition as in the Frontier, the Muslim League had a chequered history in Sind. Its difficulties stemmed from the disunity and political opportunism of the leading Muslim politicians. They were more concerned with personal rivalries and struggles for power than with political ideals and party programmes. The Sind Muslim League was consequently ill-disciplined and riven with factionalism. Its ministers pursued policies designed to keep themselves in power, even if these conflicted with the long-term aims of the parent organization. A classic example was the passage of the *Joint Electorates Bill* in April 1940. Jinnah's attempts at creating discipline seldom survived his departure from Karachi.

The Muslims' disunity carried with it the danger that the Congress might exploit the situation. A Nationalist government in Karachi might 'bury Pakistan in Sind'. The Congress, indeed, expended much money in cultivating the seamier side of Sindhi politics. The land of his ancestors proved a liability rather than an asset for Jinnah in his constitutional negotiations with the British and the Congress at the Centre. What lay behind the constant intrigues and petty bickerings of the Muslim politicians? Why did the Central Muslim League

authorities find it so difficult to discipline the wayward
Sindhis? How was the Pakistan Scheme viewed by the Sindhi
elite? This chapter attempts to answer these important
questions by shedding fresh light on the complicated political
developments in Sind during the decade which preceded
Partition. By way of background it examines the major
economic and social characteristics of the region and its
earlier history.

THE SOCIAL SETTING

The feudal character of rural Sind, the influence of *Pirs* and
Sayeds, the economic and political importance of the province's minority Hindu community, and the heterogeneous
character of its Muslim population all profoundly affected
the region's political development. The factionalism, disunity,
and particularism of Muslim politics can only be fully understood within this context.

The rural areas of Sind contained the overwhelming
majority of the province's population throughout the period
of British rule.[2] Despite the rich soils of the riverine areas
and the introduction of such cash crops as cotton and wheat,
the countryside remained backward in terms of social progress
and economic development. Houses in the *katcha*[3] area were
simple structures of wood and thatch. Water was taken from
open wells and canals. Ploughs and small agricultural imple-
ments were made of wood, as were the bullock carts still
modelled on the ancient Moenjodaro design. The sparseness
of the rural population,[4] and its poor communications[5] with
the distant towns and cities partly explains this backwardness.
Its main cause, however, was the autocratic control which the
landed elite exerted over the labourers, tenants, and petty
landowners. Their inferiority was seen in the custom of
touching the feet of 'superiors'.

The rural poor, known collectively by the term *haris*, lived
a life of total insecurity. They could be turned off the land

they cultivated at the whim of the landholder. They were subject to illegal taxes and levies and were frequently required to render forced labour. Their crops were unevenly shared with the landholder at harvest time, leaving them perpetually in debt. Tenants were constantly harried by the agents of the large landholders,[6] whilst petty landholders were forced to turn to the large landholders for physical protection. The largest landholders (waderos) kept their own armed retainers, many of whom were notorious criminals, in order to overawe the rural population. The large landholders competed amongst each other for prestige (izzat). Many of them were the chiefs (Mirs) of the Baluchi tribes which had ruled Sind before its annexation by the British. Even during the period of British rule, they continued to exert an iron grip over the haris, for the colonial authorities, in order to win their support, recognized their jagirs (revenue-free grants of land) from former times, and gave them the responsibility for the maintenance of law and order. There was thus little check on the illegal activities and oppression carried out by many landowners in order to finance their extravagant lifestyles.

Agricultural development suffered as a result of this harsh and unjust social system. The haris had no incentive to improve their cultivation methods because of their insecurity. The landholder's only interest was to squeeze as much income as possible out of their tenants and labourers. Farming efficiency and productivity remained at a low level, outside of the newly irrigated areas settled by independent peasant proprietors from the Punjab. Sind's zamindari land system was equally damaging, however, to the province's political development. The landholders brought their factional rivalries and desire for prestige and power into the arena of legislative politics. Their lack of education and frequently corrupt backgrounds lead them to be a 'destructive and immoral force'.[7] No party could, nonetheless, afford to ignore the landholders, as their power enabled them to command the votes of their haris and their wealth enabled them to buy the support of the petty *zamindars*. The mass of the rural population was so in awe of them that political organization against their wishes was almost impossible. 'It would not be a matter of days or months', the Muslim League's 1943-4 *Annual Report* noted, 'but we should require years to create political consciousness among Muslim masses in the province, where on account of long distances, scattered villages, illiteracy, and local influences, it is rather difficult to easily approach the people'.[8]

Pirs were the chief rivals to the *zamindars'* influence on the countryside. Many *pirs* were large landowners in their own right. Their power primarily rested, however, on the mass of the rural population's extreme veneration towards them and their shrines. Thirty to forty thousand people annually visited the *Urs* celebrations at the shrine of Lal Shahbaz Qalandar at Sehwan.[9] Other important shrines included those of Shah Abdul Latif at Bhit, Shah Inayat Shahid of Jhok, Shah Janullah of Rohri, and Mukhdum Muhammad Hashim of Thatta.[10] At the famous Makli Hill burial site near Thatta over 125,000 Sufi saints are reported to be buried. *Pirs* were not slow to convert their spiritual influence into political power. Syed Sibghatullah Shah of the Rashidi family, popularly known as Pir Pagaro (turbaned *Pir*), organized his absolutely obedient followers to support Ahmed Brelvi's struggle against the Sikhs in 1826. His descendants were to use their followers, known as the *Hur* (Free), in a series of struggles with the British. These were only ended after Martial Law was declared over a large area of rural Sind and the *Pir* was executed in 1943 on a charge of treason. Less dramatically, *Pirs* played a prominent role in the Khilafat Movement in Sind in 1920.[11] With the creation of first, a Sind Legislative Council and later, a Legislative Assembly, a number of *Pirs* called on the support of their devotees in order to secure election. They soon formed an important bloc within the Parliament.

The Hindu community[12] in Sind was also to have an important influence on Legislative politics, because of its high socio-economic status and the favourable weightage it received in terms of seats. The Hindus' wealth rested on their domination of trade and commerce and of the middle class professions in which access to English education was of vital importance. They also began to acquire landholdings[13] as extravagant Muslim landowners were unable to meet the loans which they had advanced. Hindu landowners did not, however, cultivate the land themselves, nor did they abandon their commercial activities, there was therefore no urban-rural split in the Hindu community as existed in neighbouring Punjab. The Hindu business classes did come into conflict with the Muslim Memon, Khoja, and Bohra traders. These Muslims were consequently more responsive to the Muslim League's appeal than the landholders. They played an important role in funding the League's early development in Sind and provided a number of its leaders.[14]

The Hindu community's wealth meant that its political representatives could buy support in the Assembly, a common feature of Sind's sordid politics. They also owned most of the press. Their opportunity for influence was also increased by the weightage afforded the Hindus by the *1932 Communal Award*. Although the Muslims made up 70 per cent of the total population, they had a bare majority (thirty-four of sixty) in the Assembly. The disunity and opportunism of many of the rural Muslim members gave the solid bloc of Hindu members considerable leverage and assured them at least one seat in every Cabinet.[15]

The heterogeneous character of the Muslim community undoubtedly hindered the aim of political unity. The Sindhi Muslims were divided by race, tribe, language, and culture. Thirty per cent of the Muslim population of Sind originated from outside its borders, although less than half this number gave a language other than Sindhi as their native tongue.[16] The immigrant groups consisted mainly of Baluchis, Sayeds, Punjabis, Memons, Khojas, and Bohras. Members from the latter three trading classes constituted virtually the entire

Muslim middle class of Sind. The bulk of the Punjabis had
settled permanently in Sind after the advent of the Jamrao
Canals in 1900 and the Sukkur Barrage Canals in 1932. They
were prosperous, independent, cultivators whose holdings
stood in marked contrast to those of the native Sindhis. Their
prosperity aroused jealousy which was to be later manipulated
by politicians in a cry against foreign domination. Perhaps,
because of the awareness of their minority status, the Punjabis
were early and ardent supporters of the Muslim League. The
Baluchis were the most important of the immigrant groups,
numbering around 23 per cent of the total Muslim population.
Baluchi shepherds and nomads from times immemorial had
left their barren mountain fastnesses to come to the fertile
Indus Valley. During the closing period of Mughal Rule and
the time of the Sindhi Kalhora rulers[17] there had been a great
influx of Baluchi settlers because governments valued their
martial qualities. The chief Baluchi tribe of Talpurs seized
power from the Kalhoras at the end of the eighteenth century,
inaugurating a period of rule by a confederacy of Baluchi
chiefs which was only ended by the British in the early 1840s.
The Talpur dynasty left the important legacy for future
political developments, of many of the largest estates and
jagirs in the region being held by Baluchi tribal chiefs.[18] The
support of the bloc of Baluchi Mir representatives was of vital
importance to any government during the period of Provincial
Autonomy, for most of the Muslim seats went to rural
constituencies. Mir Bandeh Ali Talpur, a big jagirdar of
Hyderabad and Dadu districts and a member of the Manikani
branch of the Talpur Tribe, so effectively used the Baluchi
bloc in the Assembly that he rose from a junior ministership
in April 1937 to be premier just three years later.

Another immigrant group much fewer in number than the
Baluchis, but nonetheless important because of their high
religious and social status, were the Sayeds, many of whom
had fled to Sind following the Mongol invasions in Central
Asia of the twelfth and thirteenth centuries. The religious

sanctity of many *pir* families of Sayeds led successive rulers to patronize their shrines. In this way many of the great *zamindars* and *jagirdars* of such districts as Sukkur and Nawabshah were drawn from Sayed families. Their traditional influence secured election to the new Legislatures introduced by the British. G.M. Sayed in 1937 organized a Sayed bloc in the Legislative Assembly which rivalled the *Mir* group for influence. The bewildering shifts in political alignment during the years 1937-47 owed far more to the underlying struggle for power between these groups than any trumpeted ideological considerations.

The native Sindhis comprised of persons belonging to the Rajput, Jat, Sammat, and Soomro Tribes which had existed in the region since ancient times. The bulk of the province's *haris* and agricultural service castes were drawn from this indigenous stock. The Sindhis' lowly status in their own homeland was not exploited by politicians[19] until the final stages of the Freedom Movement, although it has become an important issue in Pakistani politics. More significant in pre-Independence times was the existence of a few large Sindhi landowners who were to take their place in Legislative politics alongside the other members of the rural elite. They included such men as Ghulam Mohammed Bhurgari, Sir Shah Nawaz Bhutto, Allah Bux Soomro, and Yar Mohammed Junejo.

THE HISTORICAL BACKGROUND

The Khilafat campaign and the Sind separation movement were the two formative influences on Sindhi Muslim politics. They brought forward and shaped the outlook of many leaders who were to play a prominent role during the decade which preceded Partition.

The Khilafat campaign aroused far more enthusiasm in Sind, than neighbouring Punjab, mainly because of the backing which it received from a number of leading *Pirs*. A branch of the All-India Khilafat Conference was established in Sind in October 1919. The following May, a Provincial Conference was successfully held at Jacobabad. A *Hijrat* Committee was formed with the influential Nawabshah landowner, Yar Mohammed Junejo, as its Secretary. The All-India leadership, recognizing that Sind was a fruitful area of activity, held its annual session at Karachi in July 1921. By this date there was a network of district and subordinate committees spread throughout Sind.[20] Their establishment earned the Secretary of the Khilafat Conference of Sind, Sheikh Abdul Majid Sindhi,[21] a reputation as an effective organizer, on which he was to build a successful and influential career. Abdullah Haroon was another future Sindhi Muslim leader who first sprang to prominence through membership of the Sind Provincial Khilafat Conference. The Khilafat Movement also left an important institutional legacy in its network of branches. Significantly, when Abdul Majid Sindhi was attempting to extend the Muslim League's organization in the Hyderabad and Dadu districts in April 1938, he used the method of summoning former Khilafat committees and instructing their members to strengthen the League.[22]

The movement to separate Sind from Bombay similarly had important personal and institutional political legacies. Mohammed Ayub Khuhro and G.M. Sayed both emerged as important political figures during the key years of the separation demand, 1926-7. This period also saw growing rivalry between two Sindhi members of the Bombay Legislative Council, Shah Nawaz Bhutto, who initially opposed the demand, and Ghulam Hussain Hidayatullah. The animosity between them was to be of decisive importance in ministry formation in 1937.

Surprisingly the Muslim League did not benefit greatly from the separatism demand. The All-India League did take up the issue from 1925 onwards. But this was more as a bargaining counter to secure adequate representation for the Muslim minority provinces in any future constitutional development than out of solidarity with the Sindhi Muslims'

cause. The fact that the All-India Muslim League's Central
Council was dominated by minority area members helps to
explain this attitude. Sindhi Muslims responded to the minor
place accorded them by cold shouldering the League's organization in Sind. Leadership of the separation demand fell
instead to an umbrella organization called the Sind Azad
Conference. This was formed in September 1932. It reflected
a growing sense of regional, Muslim identity which was reinforced by the arguments the Sindhi elite advanced in their
demand for separation. The sense of a uniquely Sindhi
Muslim identity was to lie uneasily beneath the surface in the
later struggle for Pakistan.

The establishment of Sind as a separate province on 1 April
1936 signalled the end of the unity within the Muslim elite.
Disunity and factionalism were to be the hallmarks of Muslim
politics throughout the decade of Provincial Autonomy. It
was not even certain on the eve of the 1937 elections whether
the direct heir to the Azad Conference, the Sind Azad Party
of Abdul Majid Sindhi, would possess any influence in the
new Legislative Assembly.

THE 1937 SIND ELECTIONS

The Muslim League approached the 1937 Sind Provincial
Elections in as weak an organizational position as in the other
Muslim majority areas. Jinnah visited Karachi in late 1936 in
an effort to persuade Sindhi Muslim politicians to contest the
elections on the League ticket.[23] He received almost as frosty
a reception, however, as that accorded him on a similar
mission to Lahore. All he was able to achieve was a loose and
uneasy arrangement between the Sind Muslim League Parliamentary Board and the Sind Azad Party.[24] The latter organization faced stiff opposition from the Sind United Party of
Abdullah Haroon and its splinter party, the Sind Muslim
Party of Ghulam Hussain Hidayatullah.[25] The Sind United
Party patterned its appeal along the lines of Fazl-i-Husain's

non-communal, agrarian-oriented Punjab Unionist Party. In Sind, as in Punjab, however, the personal influence of the candidates counted for far more than any party programme and organization. Loyalties to clan leader, landlord, and *pir* were decisive in determining the outcome.[26] In nine of the Muslim constituencies, Sayeds and *Pirs* were elected, and in another eighteen, chieftains of tribal clans emerged victorious, including the chief of the Chandio Tribe and of the Manikani and Shahwani Talpurs. Even the two surprise defeats of Shah Nawaz Bhutto and Abdullah Haroon were the result of traditional electoral considerations, rather than party programme. Majid defeated Bhutto in his Larkana stronghold by enlisting the support of Shah Nawaz's two cousins, Nabi Baksh, the *sardar* (Chief) of Sindhi Bhuttos, and Khan Bahadur Ahmad Khan.[27] Whilst Abdullah Haroon was defeated by an Independent candidate (Khan Sahib Allah Baksh Gabol) in the Karachi city north constituency, who was able to swing the Baluch voting bloc behind him.[28]

The outcome of the 1937 elections revealed the dominance of the rural elite of large landholders, clan leaders, and *pirs*. They had secured 27 of the 34 Muslim seats. Fundamental loyalties of kinship, religion, and economic dependence counted for more than party programme. The Muslim League, therefore, had to accept these realities as it sought to establish a foothold in the region from 1938 onwards.

THE SIND MUSLIM LEAGUE 1937-40

In 1937 the Muslim League had virtually no organization in Sind and had failed to elect a single candidate on its ticket. In March 1940, however, it was on the verge of assuming power in a coalition government. Jinnah appeared to have secured a major triumph in Sind. Unfortunately for the Quaid-i-Azam this was a hollow achievement. The League's revival was not based on solid organizational development, but on the shifting sands of factional rivalries in the struggle for office.

As in other parts of India, the Muslim League made some efforts at organization in response to the threat posed by the Congress 'mass contact' campaign of 1937-8. Sheikh Abdul Majid Sindhi once again took the lead in establishing League branches in such districts as Tharparkar, Nawabshah, Sukkur, Jacobabad, and Larkana.[29] But this flurry of activity early in 1938 was limited in its impact. Progress was only possible when influential landlords such as Mohammed Ayub Khuhro gave their enthusiastic support. The League remained unable to convert the mass enthusiasm which greeted Jinnah's visit to the province in October 1938[30] into a disciplined mass base of support. Its fortunes, thus, rested on the goodwill of the rural elite, who dominated the Provincial Assembly.

The opening period of Provincial Autonomy was marked by a bewildering array of floor-crossings and shifting factional alignments, in which party loyalties counted for nothing.[31] The only constant factors were the importance of the solid blocs of *Mir* and *Sayed* members,[32] and the determination of Ghulam Hussain Hidayatullah to retain the Premiership. By March 1938, the latter had run out of possible combinations of support and was forced to resign in favour of Allah Baksh.

The formation of the Allah Baksh ministry led to an upturn in fortune for the Muslim League. Its stalwart Assembly members, Majid, Khuhro, and Gazdar, were joined in turn by such luminaries as Abdullah Haroon, Hidayatullah, and G.M. Sayed. Haroon's conversion in April 1938 was undoubtedly genuine, the result of Allah Baksh's pro-Congress leanings. Hidayatullah was prompted more by revenge and the lure of a quick return to office. G.M. Sayed, who throughout this period posed as the upholder of the *haris'* interests, was angered by a proposed increase of land revenue assessments in the Sukkur Barrage area. His inclusion in the League brought it the valuable support of the *Sayed* grouping within the Assembly. By October 1938, the newly-formed Muslim League Assembly Party could claim the support of 27 Muslim members. Allah Baksh with just six Muslim supporters clung to power, aided by the Congress and the Hindu Sabhu (known as Hindu Independents) members.

The fragile foundations of the League's new strength were cruelly exposed in the months which followed the failure to unseat Allah Baksh in October 1938. Old rivalries resurfaced and the struggle for power took precedence over consolidating the League's position. Hidayatullah was the first to defect in January 1939. He feared Abdullah Haroon's growing power as League President and willingly crossed the floor when Allah Baksh offered him a ministership. He took with him the bloc of *Mir* members, thus, overnight reducing the League to its former forlorn status. Indicative of the League's difficulties in Sind was the fact that it had to rely on the same group of *Mir* members in order to cobble together a coalition government in March 1940, following the collapse of the Allah Baksh government.

INTO GOVERNMENT

The Muslim League obtained a foothold on power in Sind, in the most inauspicious circumstances. Serious communal rioting in the Sukkur district resulting from the disputed status of the *Manzilgah* shrine had brought down the Allah Baksh governmen⁺. The Muslim League, in order to assume the reins of power, had agreed to dissolve its Assembly Party and to form a union with the Hindu Independents. The union went by the name of the Nationalist Party.[33] It also had to accept Mir Bandeh Ali as Chief Minister in order to attain the support of the *Mir* group. Khuhro, the leader of the Muslim League Assembly Party, had been so desperate to assume power and office that he had agreed to this unorthodox procedure. Both Jinnah and Haroon expressed doubts about this course of action,[34] but finally concurred. Their disquiet was soon justified, for the Muslim League ministers flagrantly disobeyed the All-India Muslim League's authority by passing an *Act* in April 1940 to introduce *Joint Electorates* for Sind's local authorities,[35] and by 'allowing Allah Baksh to return to office the following November. Both these actions stemmed from Mir Bandeh Ali's preoccupation with staying in power. He was more interested in this than the effect his behaviour might have on the status of the All-India Muslim League. Khuhro used his influence in the Assembly and the Council of the Sind Muslim League to head off any opposition to the ministry. This inevitably, but initially unsuccessfully, came from Abdullah Haroon, the League President.

Abdullah Haroon, as a member of the Working Committee of the All-India Muslim League, had a wider perspective on Muslim politics than Mir Bandeh Ali and his associates. Almost alone amongst the notable Sindhi Leaguers he sincerely supported the Pakistan demand from the outset.[36] He had presided over the Pakistan Day celebrations held in Karachi on 19 and 21 April and had addressed a meeting which followed a mammoth 10,000 strong procession through the streets.[37] He was, therefore, extremely anxious that the League's new-found popularity should not be tarnished by the opportunism of its Assembly members. The Sind Muslim League Council did not, however, share Haroon's All-India vision and in both April and July rejected his efforts to discipline the ministers. The League President now turned to a higher authority—the Quaid-i-Azam himself. His report on the situation in Sind succeeded in getting Jinnah to journey to Karachi in December 1940. He soon found that the ministers were more interested in enjoying the patronage and power of office, than building the League's strength and thus advancing the cause of Pakistan. The realities of rural power in Sind forced Jinnah, however, to work through the existing League leadership much as he would have liked to have dealt with men more loyal to his ideals. Jinnah's presence ensured that the Muslim League Assembly Party was resuscitated. It also brought a temporary halt to Khuhro's perpetual scheming. The fruits of Jinnah's diplomacy were seen in March, when the ministers dutifully stood down, rather than

desperately seeking to hold on to office, following Allah
Baksh's withdrawal of support. Allen Keith Jones maintains
that this was a major turning point in the Muslim politics of
Sind.[38] In fact it was only the opening shot in Jinnah's
struggle to exert the All-India Muslim League's authority over
the Sind Leaguers.

SIND POLITICS 1942-5 : AN OVERVIEW

Ghulam Hussain Hidayatullah formed a second Muslim League
ministry in October 1942.[39] This remained in power until the
1946 Provincial Elections. Despite the beginnings of organizational development in the rural areas, this period saw little
advance in the League's cause. Like the Aurangzeb Khan
ministry in the Frontier, Hidayatullah's government became
noted for its inefficiency and corruption. A similar struggle
also emerged between the ministers and the League's organizational wing. This was partly the traditional struggle between
the *Mirs* and the *Sayeds*. The League President, G.M. Sayed[40] ·
also injected an ideological dimension into the dispute by
claiming to uphold the interests of the *haris* and by criticizing
the ministry for its slowness in instituting agrarian reform.
The League's divisions were painfully revealed in a series of
bye-elections in late 1943 and 1944. Sayed unsuccessfully
appealed to the Working Committees of the Sind and All-India
Muslim League in July 1944. But they refused to call on the
ministers to resign. He then took the decision into his own
hands and schemed Hidayatullah's downfall. The Premier, in
order to hang on to power, was forced to take Moula Baksh
into his ministry in February 1945, although he was not a
member of the League. Jinnah was thus faced with yet
another crisis in his relations with the Sindhi leaders as
Hidayatullah's action flew in the face of official League
policy. Moreover, he had lost a valuable ally with the sudden
death of Abdullah Haroon in May 1942. Jinnah was able,
however, to bring the League Chief Minister back into line

over the issue of Moula Baksh. An example of his authority
which Ayesha Jalal conveniently overlooks in her assessment
that Jinnah was impotent and irrelevant in Sindhi politics.[41]
As the 1946 Provincial Elections approached, however, the
split between Hidayatullah and Sayed still remained. Indeed,
by 1945 there were two Leagues in existence in Sind, the
Parallel League of the Ministers, and the Sayed League.

HIDAYATULLAH ASSUMES POWER

Ghulam Hussain Hidayatullah entered office with high hopes
and grandiose premises. He agreed to work not only under
the supervision of the Muslim League Assembly Party, but
the Sind Provincial Muslim League Committee. This latter
promise was to become a major issue between him and
G.M. Sayed as the League President had packed his supporters
in the League Committee. The Premier also sketched out an
ambitious programme of agrarian reform, including legislation
on Land Alienation and Debt Redemption to curb the influence of money lenders and to increase the rights of tenants.
He further resolved to increase the proportion of Muslims in
government service and to appoint an anti-corruption
officer.[42] There was little likelihood that these reforms
would be implemented as they were not in the personal
interest of the ministers. They had come to power led not by
a reforming zeal, but by the desire for patronage and influence. 'I have an uneasy feeling', the Governor wrote to the
Viceroy shortly after Hidayatullah became Premier, 'that
almost any member would be able to form a government
with ... 12 well-paid ministerships and parliamentary secre-
taryships in his gift ... The only sensible question which one
can ask any politician is whether he is in office or out, and if
he is out, his only study is how he can get in'.[43] In such
circumstances, the ministers had little dedication to fighting
for reform. Instead, they busied themselves feathering their
own nests through the manipulation of wartime contracts

and the control of rationed and requisitioned goods.[44] Tenancy reforms were delayed and it was even suggested that there should be a modification of the limited *Jagirdari* Legislation which Allah Baksh had passed in 1941.[45]

The only bright spot of the first year of the Hidayatullah ministry was the increase in propaganda and organizational activity from April 1943 onwards. A Pakistan Conference was held in the Upper Sind Frontier District and its message was taken to the rural areas by *pirs* and *mullahs*. A membership drive throughout the province led to a sizeable increase in the number of branches and representatives.

Table 2.1: List of Branches, Members, and Representatives

Name of District	Number of Branches		Number of Members		Number of Representatives	
	1943	1944	1943	1944	1943	1944
Hyderabad	36	33	11976	40654	128	438
Tharparkar	168	272	32791	66549	366	703
Larkana	11	12	2070	2457	20	24
Nawabshah	84	53	15031	15495	150	154
Dadu	62	55	6356	6456	56	59
Jacobabad	13	20	1686	3902	14	54
Karachi	21	17	3033	3472	34	36
Sukkur	65	26	46005	13500	476	149
Karachi city	14	59	3675	24733	35	250
Total	474	547	122623	177118	1279	1865

Source: Annual Report of the Sind Provincial Muslim League for 1943-4, SHC Sind 1:24.

Even if these figures are taken at face value, they reveal that the League still had much work to do in reaching the bulk of the rural population. It is very likely, however, that they overestimate the League's advance. Many local Leaguers saw organizational work in terms of creating a power base for the capture of Legislative Assembly and District Board seats, rather than in order to advance the cause of Pakistan.[46] They would frequently enroll bogus members in order to increase their standing *vis-a-vis* their factional rivals. Fakir Muhammad Manario, in order to strengthen his position before the 1943 Muslim League elections in Tharparkar District, for example, enrolled 2,820 bogus members.[47] This was by no means an isolated incident. A more reliable guide to the Muslim League's strength than its membership figures is the fact that it still had few paid propagandists in 1944 and had to rely solely on *Alwahid*[48] to publicize its meetings and viewpoint.

THE ENEMY WITHIN

The struggle for power between the ministers and G.M. Sayed, the League President, became increasingly bitter from April 1943 onwards. The Premier received powerful backing from his former protege Khuhro and from Yusuf Haroon (Abdullah's son), who was rankled by Sayed's removal of him from the post of League Secretary. Ghulam Hussain also carried with him the *Mir* bloc within the Assembly. G.M. Sayed was backed by the *Sayed* bloc. He was also supported by Mohammad Hashim Gazdar who was at daggers drawn with Yusuf Haroon who was undermining his Karachi power base. Abdul Majid, the other leading figure in the League, briefly left its ranks to join the Azad Party after the murder of the former Premier Allah Baksh in May 1943.

The struggle began in earnest in July 1944 when Sayed called on the ministers to resign. By this date he completely controlled the League Council and Working Committee, having disqualified those branches which backed his opponents. Sayed presented his case to Jinnah in terms of the clash of interests between the large landowners of Sind and their labourers and tenants. He claimed that the ministers' support of the landed elite's interests was making the Muslim League unpopular and retarding the cause of Pakistan.[49] This charge was echoed by the submission of one of his supporters who wrote, 'Owing to the many misdeeds of the ministers ... we have been dubbed by the public as pompous propagandists who promise a lot, but do nothing substantial ... who raise slogans to catch votes ... but afterwards hibernate'.[50] Ghulam Hussain countered that Sayed was trying to bring about a 'Sayed *raj*', and he appealed to Jinnah to prevent the Sind League's disruption.[51] Neither Hidayatullah nor Sayed triumphed, as the Working Committee of the All-India Muslim League on a technicality referred the issue back to the Sind Parliamentary League.

The old wounds were reopened in December 1944, when a bye-election at Shikarpur coincided with Khuhro's arrest in connection with Allah Baksh's murder.[52] In order to make up for the loss of his Revenue Minister, the Premier attempted to secure the Shikarpur election ticket for his own son, Anwar. The Parliamentary Board, however, was dominated by Sayed's supporters and gave the ticket to his nominee. Ghulam Hussain sought Jinnah's support, but to no avail. Jinnah had no option but to back the official League candidate as he had been properly selected. The election would have been difficult for the League in any circumstances, for it was Allah Baksh's old constituency in which his family had great influence. The League's disunity made it almost inevitable that the victory would go to Moula Baksh—the murdered man's brother. Sayed predictably blamed the ministers for sabotaging the campaign. The whole affair was 'painful reading indeed' for Jinnah who bemoaned the fact that Sind's leading men were 'quarrelling amongst themselves like children'.[53] The lessons of Shikarpur were not learnt, however, because in the Tando Mohammad Khan bye-election the following month, the tug-of-war continued between the ministers and Sayed. This time, Sayed refrained from challenging the Premier's Mir candidate, but instead lent his weight to the opponent. As anticipated, the Mir candidate won, but the spectacle of disunity had dealt a further blow to the League's prestige.

Sayed now intrigued with Moula Baksh and the Hindu leader, Nichaldas Vazirani, to bring down the government.[54] He defeated the Premier in a snap vote on 23 February 1945, but had not reckoned on the Premier's long-established art of remaining in office whatever the odds. Hidayatullah, now outmanoeuvred Sayed by bringing Moula Baksh into the government, although he was not a member of the League. Jinnah responded by severely reprimanding Sayed for precipitating the crisis. He then wired Hidayatullah, telling him that his action in allowing Moula Baksh to join the Cabinet had violated the League's fundamental principles. 'Moulabux must join League immediately or else he must stand down. League honours and principles cannot be bartered away. Am most reluctant to exercise my extraordinary powers. Hoping you will stand by me, as you have done so far, and carry out my advice'.[55] Despite claims by such writers as Ayesha Jalal that Jinnah had little effective influence in Sind,[56] in this instance the Quaid-i-Azam's word was law. Moula Baksh was dropped from the ministry, despite his protests that the Premier had gone back on his word. The League organization, however, was almost irrevocably split into two, each faction possessing their local organizations and office bearers. The announcement that provincial elections would be held in the winter of 1946 signalled the final and bitter round in the contest between 'a corrupt Premier' and a 'fanatical and unsteady Provincial President'.[57]

SIND AT THE POLLS

Sind revealed most clearly the diametrically opposed attitudes of Jinnah and local Muslim politicians to the 1946 Provincial Elections. Jinnah saw them as an opportunity to pile up votes for Pakistan and thus strengthen his negotiating position with the Congress and the British. Local politicians had a more restricted and particularist view. They were primarily concerned with winning power for themselves; ministry formation took precedence over Pakistan. Hence the spectacle in Sind of the contending leaders attempting to secure tickets for their supporters with no regard for their organization's unity and prestige. Jinnah was well aware of their self-seeking outlook, but had to put up with it. For they alone had the money[58] and social influence necessary to secure election in the backward rural areas. By the end of August 1945 a three-way struggle for League tickets had broken out between Sayed, Khuhro, and Ghulam Hussain backed up by the Mirs.[59] Each were prepared to 'oppose tooth and nail' every other Leaguer who did not agree with them. Jinnah journeyed to Karachi once more to bang a few heads together. He had the sympathy of the Governor, who was equally contemptuous, 'Jinnah dislikes them all', he wrote to the Viceroy. 'He once told me he could buy the lot of them for five lakhs of rupees, to which I replied I could do it a lot cheaper'.[60] The Quaid-i-Azam realized that the best he could ask for in the circumstances was a semblance of unity and victory by candidates who owed nominal allegiance to the League. All candidates would claim support for Pakistan, but if they did not have the official League ticket, the Congress and its allies would claim a victory. Jinnah patched together a seven-member Parliamentary Board which had the responsibility of issuing the League's tickets. But as soon as his back was turned, the Committee split into two groups; a majority Hidayatullah-Mir-Khuhro axis and the minority supporters of its chairman, G.M. Sayed. Although the latter exercised his authority and adjourned the Committee, the majority continued to issue tickets. Both groups appealed to Jinnah, who once again revealed his completely opposite perspective on the elections. 'I wish people thought less of Premier and ministers and thought more of the paramount and vital issue confronting us', he admonished Khuhro, 'I do hope the seriousness of the situation will be fully realized ... The only issue before us is Pakistan *versus* Akhand Hindustan and if Sind falls, God help you'.[61] He did not, however, leave the Sindhi politicians to

THE STRUGGLES WITHIN SIND 51

their own devices, instead he suspended the Committee and despatched Liaquat Ali Khan to sort out the mess. He presided over a meeting of the Muslim League Central Parliamentary Board in Karachi which declared that G.M. Sayed's adjournment was unconstitutional.[62] The League President, however, was not the man to meekly toe the line. He issued an even greater challenge to Jinnah's authority by calling a meeting of the Provincial League Council which carried a no-confidence vote against the Parliamentary Committee.[63] There was now a real danger that the elections would turn out disastrously for the Muslim League. The Congress was known to have set aside large sums to fund the campaigns of independent Muslim candidates. The longer the uncertainty continued in the League's ranks, the more tempting the Congress money would seem. Jinnah returned to Karachi late in October and put the selection of candidates in the hands of the Central Parliamentary Board.[64] It nominated candidates favourable to the Premier. Sayed set up his own nominees as rivals to its candidates. Gazdar, seeing that expulsion from the League was inevitable, now distanced himself from Sayed. Sayed was duly ejected from the League early in January. He took with him a group of influential supporters including Mohammad Ali Shah, an ex-minister, Sayed Khair Shah and Pir Bahadar Shah of Hala, and in addition Rs. 50,000 of the League's funds, if his critics are to be believed.

Sayed's expulsion did not, however, end the dissension within the Muslim League's ranks. Ghulam Hussain complained to Jinnah that Khuhro and his agents worked against him.[65] Pir Illahi Baksh supported him in this accusation, and called for Khuhro and his friends to be ejected from the League.[66] The *Mir* group of Talpurs meanwhile had enlisted the backing of the *Khaksars* in order to ensure that they formed a powerful group in the Assembly.[67] This incongruous action was still further evidence that Pakistan meant little to the Sindhi leaders who were more concerned with winning office. Although the official League candidates routinely denounced G.M. Sayed as a traitor, their outlook was, in fact, far closer to his 'Sindhi Pakistan' scheme[68] than Jinnah's demand. For in essence all Sayed wanted was a hands-off-Sind by the central leadership. No Sindhi leader could disagree with that sentiment.

The outcome of the elections rested as usual on the personal influence of the individual candidates. Despite drafting in batches of students from Aligarh, the official League candidates could make no headway against Sayed and his followers in their home constituencies. They relied not only on their own influence in their rural domain, but also on the support of the influential *Pirs* and *Sajjada Nashins* of Hala, Jhando, and the Shrine of Shah Abdul Latif Bhit.[69]

The success of the Sayed group, together with the Congress's strong showing[70] led to a finely balanced Assembly. The Muslim League was the largest party but it was closely followed by the Sind Assembly Party Coalition of the Congress and the supporters of G.M. Sayed. The balance between them was held by a handful of independent members. Far from giving an overwhelming mandate for Pakistan, the elections had even put the limited objective of forming a Muslim League ministry in extreme jeopardy. Jinnah had to turn elsewhere in Muslim India to demonstrate backing for his Pakistan Scheme.

MUSLIM POLITICS 1946-7

The new Governor, Sir Francis Mudie, turned to the old standby Ghulam Hussain Hidayatullah to form a ministry. The Provincial League was reorganized shorn of Sayed and his supporters. They still, however, presented a danger in the Assembly where the parties were balanced on a knife's edge. For if Sayed had been able to form a pro-Congress government during the spring of 1946, it would have weakened Jinnah's position at the centre during the delicate negotiations over the *Cabinet Mission* proposals. Fortunately for the

League the ministry survived until after the collapse of the
Cabinet Mission Plan. The elections in Sind in December
1946 took place at a time when Partition appeared increasingly inevitable. Even so, the method and extent of the League's
victory was far from impressive. The League clearly had
many problems still to overcome in Sind, on the eve of the
creation of Pakistan.

The reorganization of the Sind Muslim League began early
in February 1946. Liaquat Ali Khan presided over a meeting
held at Yusuf Haroon's Karachi residence which formerly
abolished the Sind League and established a 22-member
Organizing Committee. This was headed by Gazdar and
Yusuf and was given time until May to complete its task of
enrolling new members and scrutinizing the election of local
office bearers.[71] By the end of March, the League's membership stood at 48,500. The largest contingents came from
Hyderabad District (9,875 members) and Karachi District
(7,900). In Tharparkar and Sukkur just 2,125 and 3,550 new
members had been enrolled.[72] The League had only reached
a tiny fraction of the total Muslim population.

Ghulam Hussain's ministry continued its precarious existence within the Assembly. The Congress used the power of
its purse to tempt its supporters. Khuhro, who still had his
eyes on the office of Chief Minister, was rumoured to be
intriguing with the opposition Coalition Party.[73] G.M. Sayed
played up the existing anti-Punjabi sentiment to attack the
Cabinet Mission proposals for grouping the Muslim majority
provinces in the north-west.[74] He launched bitter attacks on
Jinnah through the columns of his Sindhi newspaper
Qurbani,[75] and maintained that Sind should have nothing to
do with Punjab. Instead it should become a separate sovereign
state. By early September, the Assembly was locked in
stalemate with the ministry and its opponents, each claiming
the support of thirty members. The Governor dissolved the
Assembly and installed a caretaker Muslim League government
until fresh elections could be held. These took place early in
December.

The struggle centred on the clash between the Muslim League and the thirteen followers of Sayed.[76] The League once again called on the support of student workers from Aligarh and the Punjab. It also had the invaluable help of the Gilani *Pirs* of Multan, who had large numbers of followers scattered throughout Sind. The League was also able to make, as it did in the Frontier, a powerful and effective appeal for Muslim solidarity in the wake of the Bihar massacres.[77] It could still not, however, guarantee success in the Sayed homeland. Ghulam Hussain, therefore, welcomed with open arms four former opponents who had defected from the Sayed camp on the eve of the elections. 'People might have personal objections against these four new additions' the Premier wrote to the Central Parliamentary Board, 'but in the interests of the future of the League it is absolutely essential to accept these persons ... by their joining us the opposition are tottering with the result that each one of them is now coming to us for a League ticket'.[78] The new converts were Nabi Baksh Bhutto, the *Sardar* of the Sindhi Bhuttos, Ghulam Mohammad Bhurgri, a rich and influential *Jagirdar*, Rahim Baksh, son of the late Allah Baksh Soomro, and Pir Ali Shah, a powerful landowner who had many disciples in the Karachi east constituency. The League's strategy paid off handsomely. Nabi Baksh Bhutto was returned unopposed for G.M. Sayed's old Larkana north constituency. Rahim Baksh defeated his uncle, Moula Baksh, in the Sukkur north-west seat, whilst Pir Ali Shah overcame the Nawab of Chandio. The Sayed clique was crushed, only K.S. Khoso securing election.

Despite its success, the December elections revealed that the Muslim League still had much work to do in Sind. It continued to rely on the traditional influence of the large landholders and *Pirs* to mobilize support. The victory had been won in the name of Pakistan, but had been achieved through the local loyalties and particularism which Jinnah had opposed for so long. The commitment to the League's ideals of many of the newly-elected members was open to question. The League still lacked the organization to discipline its members. Most importantly, it was in no shape to carry out the task of nation-building once Pakistan was created. Sindhi separatism fuelled by anti-Punjabi sentiment thus found a favourable environment in which to flourish.

REFERENCE

1. Sind's agricultural prospects had been boosted by the opening of the Sukkur Barrage Scheme in 1932 which brought an additional seven million acres under cultivation. On the eve of Independence, Sind was a surplus province to the tune of some 500 million rupees.
2. Eighty-two per cent of the population lived in the countryside in 1941. *Census of India 1941*, Vol. XII, Delhi, 1942, p. 2.
3. This was the area of the wide river bed of the Indus, largely dry for most of the year and containing millions of acres of fertile land.
4. In 1931 Sind's average population density was 81 persons per square mile. In the Tharparkar district it was as low as 34. Pithawala, M.P., *An Introduction to Sind: Its Wealth and Welfare*, Karachi, 1951, p. 43.
5. Rural transport consisted of camel carts, bullock carts, and boats.
6. Landholdings in Sind were large by Indian standards. Estates of 20,000 to 30,000 acres were not uncommon.
7. Memorandum of G.M. Sayed, 11 June 1943, SHC Sind 1:5.
8. *Annual Report of the Sind Provincial Muslim League for 1943-4,* SHC Sind 1:24.
9. Smyth, J.W., *Gazetteer of Sind*, B, Vol. IV, Larkana, Bombay, 1919, p. 47.
10. This Naqshbandi saint led a campaign at the beginning of the eighteenth century to bring Sindhi Sufism more in line with orthodox practice.
11. Pir Taj and Pir Turab Ali Shah were important members of the Sind Provincial Khilafat Conference which was held in February 1920.
12. The Hindus numbered 28 per cent of the population, unlike in neighbouring Punjab, they did not form the majority in any district, although they had a virtual equality with the Muslims in Tharparkar.
13. Thirty-one per cent of the total occupied area in Sind was in Hindu hands by the 1920s. Covernton, S.H., *Report on the Subject of Legislation to Restrict the Alienation of Land in Sind by Members of the Agricultural Classes,* Karachi, 1927, p. 19.
14. Most notably Abdullah Haroon, who was a prominent Memon sugar merchant. Hatim Alavi, who was at one time Mayor of Karachi, was a Bohra businessman. Another leading Leaguer, Muhammad Hashim Gazdar, was a Karachi contractor.
15. It is debatable whether the Muslim disunity in the Assembly during the period of Provincial Autonomy was a consequence of the Hindus' over-representation or would have occurred any way.
16. Baluchi, Punjabi, Gujarati, Hindi, and Rajasthani were the other major languages.
17. They were semi-independent rulers of Sind from 1736 onwards. By the end of the eighteenth century they had been overthrown by the Talpurs.
18. The Jatois held large estates in Sukkur, for example, the *Sardar* (Chief) of the Chandio Tribe owned vast estates in Larkana District, descendants of the Talpurs owned land at Mirpurkhas in Tharparkar District.
19. G.M. Sayed was the first to fully take up this issue.

20. Jones, A.K., 'Muslim Politics and the Growth of the Muslim League in Sind 1935-1941', Unpublished thesis, Duke University, 1977, p. 58.
21. Majid was a convert from Hinduism. He moved from Thatta to Hyderabad after being disowned by his family and took up a career as a journalist.
22. Jones, op. cit., 1977, p. 147.
23. Ibid., p. 71.
24. Ibid., pp. 60-72.
25. The Sind Muslim Party was backed by the influential Junejo, Jatoi, and Khuhro families. Its ideology was identical to its parent Sind United Party. It owed its existence solely to the inability of Hidayatullah and Shah Nawaz Bhutto to work within the same party.
26. Less than one in ten Sindhis voted in the elections.
27. Jones, op. cit., 1977, p. 108.
28. The constituency included the Lyari quarter with its large Baluch and Pathan immigrant worker population. Ibid., p. 110.
29. Jones, op. cit., 1977, p. 146.
30. Jinnah had come to preside over the First Sind Provincial Muslim League Conference. His arrival in Karachi had led to scenes of great enthusiasm. He was conveyed through the streets in a three-mile procession in a manner 'befitting a king'.
31. The Sind Muslim Party of Ghulam Hussain Hidayatullah had captured just four seats in the elections, but its number soon swelled to 28, at the expense of the Sind United Party, when it became clear that Hidayatullah was the favourite of the British Governor for the post of Premier.
32. Hidayatullah had relied on the Mir members to form his ministry. They included Mir Bandeh Ali, Mir Ghulam Ali Khan, Mir Muhammad Khan Chandio, Kaiser Khan Bozdar, Mir Zenuldin Sunderani, Allah Baksh Gabol, Sohrab Khan Sarki, and Jaffer Khan Burdi. The rival Sayed group consisted of Miran Mohammad Shah, G.M. Sayed, Muhammad Ali Shah, Ghulam Hyder Shah and Khairshah.
33. Jones, op. cit., 1977, p. 205 and ff.
34. Graham to Linlithgow, 16 February 1940, p. 57, Linlithgow Papers, MSS, Eur F 125/96 IOR.
35. This had been part of the 21 part programme agreed with the Hindu Independents before the Ministry was formed. It was a direct response to the communal violence in the Sukkur District.
36. Graham to Linlithgow, 1 July 1940, L/P&J/5/255 IOR.
37. Sind FR, second half of April 1940, L/P&J/5/255 IOR.
38. Jones, op. cit., 1977, p. 244.
39. The Governor had dismissed Allah Baksh as he believed he no longer carried the support of the Assembly.
40. He was elected President in June 1943, after Jinnah had forced Khuhro to step down as he ruled that no member of the ministry could hold office in the organization.
41. Jalal, A., The Sole Spokesman, Jinnah, The Muslim League and the Demand for Pakistan, Cambridge, 1985, p. 113.
42. S.F. Kucchi, member of Working Committee of Sind Provincial Muslim League to G.M. Sayed, SHC Sind 11:37.
43. Dow to Linlithgow, 5 November 1942, L/P&J/5/258.
44. S.F. Kucchi, member of Working Committee of Sind Provincial Muslim League to G.M. Sayed, SHC Sind 11:37.
45. This had introduced Survey Settlement in the unsettled areas of the jagirs and substituted a payment of land revenue for a crop-sharing arrangement between the jagirdars and cultivators.
46. Annual Report of the Sind Provincial Muslim League for 1943-4, SHC Sind 1:24.
47. Letter of K.S. Ghulam, K.B. Ghulam Nabi Shah, K.B. Ghulam Hussain, and Sayed Ghulam Hydar Shah to Jinnah. NO FMA Sind Muslim League, Part IV, 1942-3, File 381.

48. This was a Sindhi daily founded by Abdullah Haroon and for many years associated with Sheikh Abdul Majid Sindhi.
49. G.M. Sayed to Jinnah, 8 July 1944, SHC Sind 1:44.
50. S.F. Kucchi, member of Working Committee of Sind Provincial Muslim League to G.M. Sayed, SHC Sind 11:37.
51. Ghulam Hussain to Jinnah, 7 July 1944, SHC Sind 1:6.
52. The fact that Khuhro was a leading suspect speaks volumes concerning the moral character of Sindhi politics. Khuhro was acquitted, although hardly exonerated, in August 1945. On his release, Yusuf Haroon garlanded him with gold sovereigns.
53. Jinnah to Ghulam Hussain, 26 December 1944, SHC Sind IV:5.
54. Sayed's opponents claimed his support for the downtrodden had been a pretence all along and that he was really in the pay of the Congress. Letter from Sind Muslim League Publicity Officer to Gazdar, 4 February 1946, Sind Provincial Muslim League, Part IX, 1946-7, FMA.
55. Telegram of Jinnah to Ghulam Hussain Hidayatullah, 2 March 1945, SHC Sind V:34.
56. Jalal, op. cit., 1985.
57. Hatim A. Alavi to Jinnah, 6 February 1945, SHC Sind IV:9.
58. It was reckoned to cost each candidate Rs. 25,000 to Rs. 50,000 to secure election, Sind FR, 5 September 1945, L/P&J/5/261 IOR.
59. All three wanted a solid bloc of supporters, in order to make a bid for the Premiership, Gazdar to Jinnah, 21 August 1945, SHC Sind VI:23(1).
60. Dow to Wavell, 20 September 1945, L/P&J/5/261 IOR.
61. Jinnah to Khuhro, 13 October 1945, SHC Sind Vol. VI:10.
62. FR, 15 October 1945, L/P&J/5/261 IOR.
63. FR, first half of October 1945, L/P&J/5/261 IOR.
64. Its members from other provinces understood less about the intricacies of Sind politics 'than a crocodile does about algebra', the Governor maintained. Sind FR, first half of October 1945, L/P&J/5/281 IOR.
65. Ghulam Hussain telegram to Jinnah, 19 January 1946, SHC Sind 7:42.
66. Pir Illahi Baksh to Liaquat Ali Khan, 2 January 1946, SHC Sind 7:33.
67. Makhdum Abdur Rashid Arshad to Jinnah, 14 January 1946, SHC Sind 7:36.
68. Sayed began to publicly voice this demand in November 1945. He linked the All-India leadership's 'interference' in Sind with the domination of the 'corrupt' members and jagirdars.
69. Mohammad Shah Saleh to President Sind Muslim League ND, SHC Sind 8:33.
70. Congress won 79 per cent of the Hindu vote and 16.6 per cent of the total vote. The Muslim League won 60 per cent of the Muslim vote and 46 per cent of the total.
71. Report of meeting held on 7 February 1946, Sind Muslim League, Part IX, 1944-6, Vol. 386, FMA.
72. Minutes of the meeting of the Organizing Committee of the Sind Provincial Muslim League, 27 March 1946, Sind Muslim League, Part IX, 1944-6, Vol. 386, FMA.
73. Jalal, op. cit., 1985, p. 219.
74. Mudie to Wavell, 24 March 1946, L/P&J/5/262 IOR.
75. See, for example, the issue for 11 June 1946. Sind Muslim League, Part IX, 1944-6, Vol. 386, FMA.
76. Fifteen Congressmen and four Muslim Leaguers including Khuhro were returned unopposed.
77. Hartal had been observed in Karachi on 15 November to mark Bihar Day. Accounts of what had happened in Bihar formed a prominent part of the League's election addresses. Mudie believed that the election results were 'Sind's answer to Bihar', FR, 14 December 1946, L/P&J/5/262 IOR.
78. Ghulam Hussain Hidayatullah to members of the Central Parliamentary Board, 17 October 1946, SHC Sind 8:26.

3
The League's Battle in Bengal

Bengal, with its 33 million Muslims, was a key area in Indian Muslim politics. At the time of Partition, about one in three Muslims lived within its borders. Although Bengal's distinctive cultural and linguistic traditions marked it off from the Muslim areas of North India, historically it had been closely connected with the cause of Muslim separatism. Hindu opposition to Lord Curzon's partition of the province in 1905 had provided the catalyst for the inauguration of the All-India Muslim League in Dacca in 1906. It was to subsequently hold more annual sessions in Bengal than any other Muslim majority area.

The Muslim League's development in Bengal during the pre-Partition decade shared many common features with its experience elsewhere in Muslim India. The League Assembly members constantly intrigued against each other in the scramble for power. The familiar conflict occurred between the ministers and party organizers with the former being taken to task for 'mere electioneering' and for standing in the way of wider-ranging social and economic reform. Nazimuddin's ministry from March 1943 onwards was no more able to deal with the acute problems brought by the war than Aurangzeb Khan's in the Frontier, or Ghulam Hussain's in Sind. It too was charged as corrupt and inefficient by League officials.

There were also, however, significant differences between the League's position in Bengal and the other majority areas. Bengal was the only province in which the League could claim a share of power after the 1937 elections. The League was able to neutralize its Muslim opponents in Bengal far earlier than in Punjab or the Frontier. It was also able to build a real mass organization in a number of districts, by 1945. In the other Muslim majority areas it had no success at all in the task of institutionalizing the support for its ideals.

This chapter attempts to shed fresh light on the Muslim League's growth in Bengal. It assesses the potentialities and problems this presented for Jinnah. Attention has been drawn to the way in which the League's development in Bengal differed from elsewhere in Muslim India. A brief background is provided before turning to the 1937 elections.

THE MUSLIMS OF BENGAL

The bulk of the Muslim population of Bengal consisted of illiterate tenants and landless labourers who were centred in the northern and eastern districts of the province. The land transfers of the late eighteenth century, together with the loss of opportunity for military service, had decimated the old Muslim elite of the Mughal era.[1] The Muslim cultivators were stripped of their customary rights by the *1793 Permanent Settlement* which gave the predominantly Hindu *zamindars* proprietary rights to their lands.[2] Shorn of their security of tenure, the Muslim cultivators' status was further depressed by the rise in population during the nineteenth century.[3] Many became heavily indebted to Hindu moneylenders in order to raise cash to pay rent and buy grain. Landownership and moneylending converged into a single interwoven complex, as moneylenders acquired land, and high caste *zamindars*[4] set up moneylending businesses. *Marwari* moneylenders also moved into the jute trade of northern Bengal. Some Muslims were rent receivers, notably old established landowning families such as the Nawabs of Dacca, and a growing class of wealthy *jotedar* tenureholders, in such areas as the Noakhali District.[5] But they were too few in number to affect the agrarian structure's provision of the basis for a communal political divide. Demands for the Abolition of the Permanent Settlement, a curbing of the landlords' influence, and for an improvement in the lot of the peasantry became central themes in Muslim politics during the 1930s and 40s. The Congress which had already alienated Muslims during the *Swadeshi* movement of 1906-8, lost all credibility with them, when it stood up for the landlords' rights at the time of the *1928 Bengal Tenancy Act.* Increasingly within the Muslim heartland of East Bengal, the politics of agrarian reform and of communalism became intertwined.

The Muslims' social backwardness together with their clinging to traditional education in religious colleges (*madrassas*) meant that they lagged far behind the high caste Hindus in English education. Just one in ten persons employed in government service were Muslim. Over half the appointments were held by Brahmins, Baidyas, and Kayasthas. 'Bengali society', the *Bengal District Administration Committee Report, 1913-14* noted, 'was a despotism of caste, tempered by matriculation'.[6] Modern Muslim education[7] was strictly limited in scope, it had produced by the eve of the First World War a small professional elite of Bengali speaking lawyers and journalists who came from a rural background. Their most famous representative was Fazlul Huq. Such men were to play a leading role in introducing political organization for the peasantry. A generation later the graduates of Dacca University[8] were to make a major contribution to the Pakistan Movement. Like Fazlul Huq before them, they sought to wrest the leadership of the Muslim community from the landed aristocracy and their Calcutta business allies.

Although the Muslim *zamindars* of East Bengal were few in number, they played an influential role in Muslim politics. The Nawab family of Dacca which traced its origins to Kashmir, provided for over thirty years leaders for the Bengal Muslim League. Indeed, its influence was so great that it supplied two of the seven Muslim ministers in the League ministry of 1943.[9] Another family member (Nawab Nasrullah) was a parliamentary secretary. The family drew its allies from the business magnates of Calcutta.[10] The Bengal Muslim

League, in fact, owed its organization in 1936 to two Calcutta businessmen, Ispahani and Abdur Rahman Siddiqui. It also received much of its funding from this quarter.

The Calcutta business community shared with the East Bengal *zamindars* a common immigrant status and an attachment to the Urdu cultural world. Both tended to regard themselves as superior to the 'Hinduized' Bengali speaking peasants,[11] as also did the immigrant Muslim industrial workers of Calcutta.[12] Although the rural Muslim population of Bengal shared some Hindu superstitions and practices such as the worship of *Sitala,* the goddess of smallpox, this was also common in other Muslim areas of India. It would be misleading to draw too sharp a contrast between an orthodox Urdu cultural world and a heterodox Bengali one. The reformist movements of Hajji Shariat-Allah and Titu Mir had bitten deep into the countryside in the early nineteenth century,[13] whilst Bengali Sufism had been regenerated later by the activities of Maulana Karamat Ali Jaunpuri (d. 1873).[14] Islamic revival added a cultural divide to the economic gulf which separated Bengali Muslims from their Hindu counterparts.[15] The conditions were consequently less favourable for cross-communal political co-operation in Bengal than in the other major Muslim area of Punjab.

THE 1937 BENGAL ELECTIONS

The Muslim League's performance in the 1937 Bengal elections was markedly superior to that in any of the other majority areas. In Punjab, the League ended up with one seat. Sind and the Frontier went to the polls with no Muslim League presence. In Bengal, however, the League captured thirty-nine of the eighty-two seats contested, and emerged as the leading Muslim party. It won three more seats than its Krishak Praja Party rival, although it polled fewer votes, (27 per cent of the total Muslim vote, compared with the Praja Party's 31 per cent). The League was thus in a position to form a ministry

in the Legislature, although much depended on the attitude
of the large number.of Independent Muslims (some forty-two
in all) and on that of the Congress, which was the single
largest party. What lay behind the Muslim League's relative
success in Bengal, for its organization had been as inert there
in the early 1930s as in any of the other majority provinces?

The crucial difference between the situation in Bengal and
that in Sind and the Punjab was that Jinnah succeeded in
bringing an influential, political grouping under the wing of
the League's Parliamentary Board. Whilst the Punjab Unionist
Party, Sind Muslim Party, and the United Party rejected his
overtures, the United Muslim Party of Bengal agreed to take
over the mantle of the moribund Muslim League. All of the
League's candidates in the elections were drawn from the old
United Muslim Party.[16] Its entry into the League's ranks gave
Jinnah access both to the money and organizational skills[17]
of the Calcutta businessmen and to the traditional influence
of the Nawabs and *zamindars* of East Bengal.[18] The Muslim
landowners had turned down an earlier chance of uniting
with Fazlul Huq's Krishak Praja Party[19] because of its radical
social demands. They saw the League's communal appeal as a
useful adjunct to their traditional influence.[20] The election
was not, however, fought simply in terms of a straightforward
religious appeal *versus* an economic one. The Muslim League
too claimed to be concerned about the lot of peasants and
workers. Indeed, at a meeting held in Barisal, its supporters
claimed it was the real Praja Party.[21] Such assertions were
not entirely unconvincing, as a number of prominent peasant
organizers, such as Akram Khan, Tamizuddin Khan, and
Abdur Rahim, had joined its ranks. The local support and
organization such workers brought was evidenced in the
Muslim League's success in District Board elections in
Mymensingh and Barisal on the eve of the Assembly
elections.[22] The Krishak Praja Party, for its part, not only
relied on such slogans as the abolition of *zamindari* and food
for everyone, but also utilized the traditional influence of

smaller landowners and *pirs*, who distributed *fatwas* in its favour. Bengal's most influential *Pir*, however, Shah Sufi Maulana Abu Bakr, the *Pir* of Furfura Sharif, threw his weight behind the Muslim League. Even this was not sufficient to prevent Khwaja Nazimuddin's defeat at Huq's hands in the *zamindari* heartland of Patuakhali. This was by far the most sensational result of the elections.

The other seats in the Nawab family's Dacca preserve went to the Muslim League as expected. Its other main areas of success were in the urban constituencies and the West Bengal constituencies of the Nadia, 24-Parganas and Bankura districts. The Krishak Praja Party succeeded primarily in the eastern Districts of Khulna, Jessore, Mymensingh, and Faridpur, which had been the main centres of the Praja (Tenant) movement for a considerable time.

THE HUQ MINISTRY OF 1937-41

The Muslim League shared power in a coalition government headed by Fazlul Huq from the 1937 elections until December 1941. During this period its power greatly increased at the expense of the Chief Minister and his Krishak Praja Party. Huq found it possible only to introduce a limited programme of agrarian reform. This alienated his own followers who wanted more radical measures, at the same time as adding credibility to the League's claims that it cared for the interests of all Bengali Muslims. Many Krishak Party members deserted Huq, bitter at the compromises he had been forced to make. The Chief Minister increasingly became the prisoner of the Muslim League. Jinnah was able to secure Huq's backing at the 1937 Lucknow Muslim League session on his own terms,[23] and to impose his control from the centre on the Bengali President's support for the British war effort. Whilst the Krishak Praja Party began to disintegrate, the Muslim League made its first tentative steps during this period to build a mass base of support.

Huq's problems began at the outset of his ministry. In order to secure the Muslim League's backing,[24] he allotted it four of the six Muslim posts in the government.[25] This decision embittered many of the Krishak Praja Party Assembly Members who had fought a fierce campaign against the *zamindars* only to see them elevated to a position where they could dilute any programme of agrarian reform. Local activists attempted to pressurize the government by organizing a series of conferences in East Bengal in which there was much 'wild talk' and 'communistic propensities' displayed.[26] When Huq appeared unmoved, Shamsuddin Ahmed, the Secretary of the Krishak Praja Party, and twenty other 'left wing' members, deserted the government which they claimed had gone back on its election promises. A local Krishak Conference held in the Rangpur District backed up their decision by passing a vote of no-confidence in the Chief Minister.[27] Huq retaliated by calling a meeting of the Krishak Praja Assembly Party in which he expelled 17 members and ensured that new office bearers loyal to himself were elected. Whilst this action restored party discipline, it left Huq with a very precarious majority. Aware of this and Government House's preference for Nazimuddin as Chief Minister, he travelled to Lucknow in October 1937 to pledge his support for Jinnah at the Centre in return for a helping hand in the locality. Jinnah's claim that the League represented all India's Muslims received a major boost with the open backing of the Bengal President. Huq, for his part, was ensured of a further stay in office, but he had lost his independence.

The landlord members of the government showed where their real interests lay when they forced Huq to agree to a Commission of Enquiry into the Permanent Settlement rather than abolish it. More limited reforms were forthcoming, and the improvements they brought in the lot of the peasantry raised the Muslim League's status in the countryside. The main legislative measures were: *Bengal Tenancy Act, 1938, Agricultural Debtors Act, 1940, Bengal Money Lenders Act, 1944,* and *Bengal Secondary Education Bill, 1940.*

Similar measures were being passed in Punjab and Bihar, during this same period, to curb the influence of money-lenders and increase tenants' rights. The *Tenancy Act* was particularly popular[28] as it made illegal many landlord exactions and cesses and reduced the interest rate on arrears of rent from 12.5 to 6.5 per cent.[29]

Jinnah's increased influence in Bengali Muslim politics was seen in May 1938 when he induced some of the followers of Tamizuddin Khan, who had deserted the government in March, to return to the fold.[30] Huq was by this time very much under the control of his League colleagues who were quick to stamp on any signs of his attempting to break free.[31] He was thus relieved when the question of Muslim League membership of District War Committees surfaced in June 1940. For here was an issue on which he could take an independent stance, sure of British sympathy and of support from the more conservative Muslim Leaguers.[32] Huq's victory in this preliminary skirmish emboldened him to publicly break with Jinnah in July 1941 over membership of the Viceroy's Executive Council. His resignation from the League sparked off demonstrations in Calcutta orchestrated by Suhrawardy. The Governor, John Herbert, attempted to reconcile Huq[33] with Suhrawardy and Nazimuddin, but the crisis ended in all the Cabinet ministers tendering their resignations. After a period of some uncertainty, Huq returned to power at the head of a Progressive Coalition Assembly Party. It included Sarat Bose's Forward Bloc Congressmen, various Krishak Praja Party men, scheduled caste members, and Hindu Mahasbhites. Their hated leader, Shyma Prasad Mookerji, became Minister of Finance. By including him, Huq laid himself open to charges of treachery and anti-Muslim sentiment. The Muslim League was able to take full advantage of this miscalculation, because of the strides it had taken in organization since 1937.

The League was initially stirred into action by the Congress mass contact campaigns in the Noakhali, Dacca, and Tippera districts. It responded by creating new branches at Comilla in December 1937.[34] The following month, Muslim students held in Comilla a large anti-Congress rally.[35] The League held a successful session in Calcutta early in May 1938 which was attended by Jinnah. Immediately afterwards, organizational activity was stepped up in the Murshidabad District.[36] The League's advance was made easier by the popularity of the *Bengal Tenancy Act* and by the programme of rural reconstruction carried out by local branches, whilst in the industrial areas of Calcutta, Suhrawardy formed union organizations to fight for improved working conditions.[37]

THE LEAGUE IN OPPOSITION 1943

During his second ministry of December 1941 to March 1943, Fazlul Huq attempted to build a cross-communal coalition similar to that which ruled the Punjab. The basic economic antagonisms between the Muslim and Hindu communities would have made this difficult at any time. The strains and stresses of the war at a time when Bengal was the frontier in the war with Japan, and the outbreak of communal disturbances as recently as April 1941 in the Dacca, Khulna, and Noakhali Districts made this an impossible task. Huq also struggled to restore the impetus of the Krishak Praja movement. Many of its members had become disillusioned by the factional struggles which had broken out during the Huq-League coalition ministry. The legislative measures which had been passed had also taken some of the heat out of demands for agrarian reform. Huq's Machiavellian alliance with Shyma Prasad Mookerji, although it was shortlived,[38] further cost him support amongst Muslim Prajas. From 1945 onwards, therefore, there was a constant trickle of ex-Krishak Praja members into the Muslim League's ranks. It was to become a torrent following the July 1945 Simla Conference.

The Muslim League vigorously took up the challenge of breaking Huq's ministry. In the Assembly, it engineered a succession of no-confidence motions, whilst outside it organized a series of demonstrations designed to unnerve the Chief Minister. Early in 1942, Suhrawardy and Nazimuddin made an extensive tour of eastern and northern Bengal to carry out propaganda against the Huq ministry. They denounced Huq as a traitor to Islam. Black Flag demonstrations were organized to greet the Chief Minister wherever he went. Under the weight of these attacks, Huq was 'showing increasing signs of nervous activity'.[39] The League also stepped up its Pakistan propaganda. A Pakistan deputation toured the Barbhanga District in January 1942, whilst an audience of over 5,000 was attracted to a Pakistan meeting held in Chittagong on 20 January.[40] Further pressure was put on Huq by organizing a League membership drive in his home Barisal District. This was so successful that a League activist could boast to Jinnah that over 160,000 members had been enrolled.[41]

The League's campaign against the ministry eventually led the Governor to force Huq to resign. He was concerned that the divisions in the Muslim community were hindering the war effort. The Muslim ministers were, in fact, reluctant to tour the districts to 'strengthen public morale'[42] because they would be greeted by black flag demonstrations. When Huq did venture out of Calcutta he was more concerned with strengthening his support than promoting the war effort. John Herbert greeted Huq's resignation with relief. 'Huq and Huq's ministry' he confided to the Viceroy, 'were a menace to good government and to security'.[43]

RETURN TO POWER

The Muslim League's assumption of office in the spring of 1943 led to a further influx of Huq's supporters into its ranks. Henceforth, it had no serious challenge to its dominance. This did not mean, however, that all was plain sailing. The League ministry had to deal with the appalling problems brought by the Bengal famine and take some of the blame for them. The struggle for supremacy between the old guard led by Nazimuddin and Suhrawardy[44] increased in intensity with the prize of the Chief Ministership at stake. The situation differed from that in Sind, however, in that a third powerful figure emerged standing outside the two factions. This was Abul Hashim, who was the League's Secretary. Whilst Suhrawardy increasingly eroded Nazimuddin's position within the existing League organization, Abul Hashim, backed up by an enthusiastic band of Dacca students, sought to extend it within the rural areas. By 1945, Abul Hashim had succeeded in building up the most effective District League organization anywhere in India. Although he was the first to admit that much work was still to be done.

The changes brought by Suhrawardy and Abul Hashim greatly strengthened the Bengal League. They were, however, a mixed blessing as far as Jinnah was concerned. His relations with Nazimuddin had always been more cordial than with Suhrawardy whom he did not entirely trust. Suhrawardy, moreover, had also elbowed aside the Quaid's Calcutta business supporters, including his close confidant, Ispahani, thus reducing his flow of information from the Bengal League. Abul Hashim's work in the localities also brought its problems. It was undoubtedly successful in winning over rural support, including many Krishak Praja activists. But it stressed Pakistan as holding the key to the peasants' immediate economic and social problems.[45] Pakistan was spoken of in almost millenial terms as the answer to all oppression and poverty.[46] This was all very well in helping the League win power, but Jinnah was well aware that the unrealistic expectations it was arousing amongst the oppressed peasantry was storing up difficulties for the future.

THE MUSLIM LEAGUE AND THE BENGAL FAMINE

The Bengal famine caused a loss of over two million lives.[47] Its basic causes, the loss of imports of rice with the Japanese occupation of Burma, and the collapse of the transport system in Bengal,[48] could not be blamed on the Nazimuddin ministry. Nor could the indifference of the British government in sending food imports, despite the Viceroy's pleas.[49] Of course, the League government must share some of the responsibility for a catastrophe which at its peak saw a daily influx into Calcutta of 700 destitute men, women, and children.[50] The ministry was, for example, slow in rationing food in Calcutta and establishing refugee camps there. Nor did it clamp down hard enough on those caught pilfering and misappropriating foodstuffs. Its opponents, however, were not only quick to point out these weaknesses, but to heap the whole of the blame for the disaster on the luckless ministers.

The 'entire' press were against the ministry, and according to the Governor, were deliberately 'spreading despondency and panic' with a view to discrediting it.[51] The opposition, after a three-day Assembly debate on the food situation, unsuccessfully brought a vote of no-confidence against Nazimuddin. Shyma Prasad Mookerjee voiced the Hindu traders' growing anger at Suhrawardy's[52] seizure of food stocks and closure of warehouses.[53] Fazlul Huq, however, made the most dramatic protest against the ministry when he called upon 20,000 students to march to Nazimuddin's house and 'demand food'.[54] The League leaders could hardly complain about their opponents' exploitation of wartime distress in order to undermine their position, as its Punjab branch was using exactly the same tactics against the Unionist government. Jinnah was sufficiently concerned, however, to rule that the League's officials were not to hold government posts as well.[55] For the same reason, it was hardly a setback when the ministry fell from office in March 1945, as the League organization could no longer be blamed for unpopular government policies. Moreover, it could concentrate its energies on preparation for future provincial elections.

LOCAL DEVELOPMENTS 1943-5

The struggle between Suhrawardy and Nazimuddin came into the open at the Bengal League's 1943 session. Whilst Nazim-uddin controlled the Muslim League Assembly Members, Suhrawardy had far more influence in the Party outside[56] it. His power rested amongst the workers and petty businessmen of Calcutta. They supported him, thanks largely to his labour organization, but also, in part, because of the reputation he had earlier acquired as Secretary of the Khilafat Movement. This Calcutta base gave Suhrawardy a powerful voice in League affairs, as district membership of the League Council was decided on a population basis. Suhrawardy's home district had the maximum weightage.

The 1943 session saw the beginning of Suhrawardy's eclipse of the Nazimuddin faction which culminated in his assuming the Premiership in April 1946. His nominees secured the posts of Vice-Presidents and Assistant Secretaries, and made up the whole of the Bengali delegation to the All-India Muslim League's Council.[57] Nazimuddin was dealt a further blow by Abul Hashim's independent attacks on his Dacca allies. The Dacca League had traditionally been in the pocket of the Nawab family. Nazimuddin's younger brother, Shahab-uddin, was its President, his cousin was its Secretary.[58] Any organization it possessed was purely on paper. When the Dacca League held its first ever elections in September 1944 at Abul Hashim's behest, Shahabuddin was confident that his nominees would be returned. 'The masses and the intelligent-sia were so bitterly against him' that all of his candidates were, however, defeated in a 'sensational' election.[59] The days of the oligarchs appeared to have passed.

Abul Hashim's drive to democratize the Dacca League was part of his general policy. A long tour of eastern Bengal between April and June 1944 convinced him of the 'complete amateurishness' of the League's District organization.[60] 'The entire activity of a District unit', he noted, 'is confined in most cases to abstract general propaganda among the masses about the League being the only platform for the Muslims and the running of the elections to the District Boards and such other bodies'.[61] The heart of the problem lay in the 'definite resistance on the part of the District leaders against building the League. They have a lurking fear in their mind that if these organizations were democratized and strengthened, their leadership ... might be eliminated. In their anxiety to retain their age-long vested interests they are fast becoming a dead-weight and retarding the growth of the League'.[62] Dacca showed the way forward. By the end of 1944 its District Muslim League had a membership of over 100,000 and had secured the uncontested election of all of its candidates in the School Board elections.[63] A rapid growth in membership also occurred in the Tippera and Barisal districts.[64] The final provincial total for the enrolment of new members during 1944 was 550,000.[65] Enthusiasts hailed this rising tide of support as 'revolutionary' and rejoiced in the fact that the League had become a 'really mass movement'.[66] Abul Hashim, however, did not rest so easily on his laurels. Whilst he took satisfaction in the fact that the League's membership exceeded 'the number ever scored by any organization in the province' including the Congress, he was well aware that this was 'but a minor achievement' compared with 'the large Muslim population of the province owing allegiance to the League and yet out of its organizational fold'.[67]

Hashim's successful campaign created increasing tension with the ministerialist group. Only the Agriculture Minister showed any enthusiasm for enrolling new members.[68] Nazimuddin, smarting at his defeat in Dacca, encouraged his agents to put around the propaganda that Hashim and his student followers were 'Communists'.[69] Hashim retorted that the ministers were running a parallel League and that their 'unbridled favouritism and nepotism' had 'evoked disgust in every honest League member'.[70]

Abul Hashim's democratization process extended to the Bengal League's constitution. Its Working Committee became a more open and representative body as the President's powers of nomination were cut down, whilst the districts were given more say in the League Council. Both organizations sprang to life. The Working Committee held an un-precedented 22 sessions during 1944, none of which 'elapsed owing to want of quorum',[71] whilst there was a record attend-ance at the Bengal Council Meeting held in Calcutta in November 1944. Delegates and Members came from every district, including large numbers of students who had 'sold their books' to pay their rail fare. They had come to support Abul Hashim in what promised to be a trial of strength with the old guard.

A major row erupted before the proceedings had got underway, when the League President, Maulana Akram Khan, acting on Nazimuddin's behalf, proposed in a meeting of the Working Committee that the larger Council meeting be cancelled.[72] (The Nazimuddin faction had done their sums and concluded that they were outnumbered on the Council.) The Maulana failed in this cynical manoeuvre, and was, henceforth, greeted with cries of 'shame' whenever he addres-sed the Council, whilst Abul Hashim was 'lustily cheered and applauded'.[73] A split similar to that which later occurred in the Sind League appeared on the cards. Suhrawardy managed to avert this, however, by cobbling together a com-promise which left the ministerialists in a majority on the Working Committee, but ensured that in future no member of the Assembly would have ex-officio rights to League membership unless he was returned by a District League.[74] Akram Khan and Abul Hashim embraced and proposed each other for the posts of League President and League Secretary respectively. An emotional scene ensued in which Suhrawardy 'overwhelmed with feelings of joy, began weeping and fell down', whilst Nazimuddin was also 'all the time weeping'.[75]

The Council meeting's outcome enabled Hashim to carry on with his mass membership drive. Muslim League meetings were held in the Murshidabad, Rangpur, Noakhali, and Rajshahi districts early in 1945.[76] Local branches were estab-lished within every union of the Rajshahi district. Successful conferences were organized in the Burdwan district and Greater Calcutta. Nearly 50,000 people attended the latter conference, giving further evidence of the League's growing appeal.[77] Hashim devoted special attention to Fazlul Huq's home district which contained nine Assembly seats. By the end of 1945, it boasted the largest League membership of any district in India, with over 300,000 members.[78]

At the same time as the Muslim League was extending its activities in the localities, Nazimuddin's power in the Assembly was waning. His ministry's actions were no more unpopular than they had ever been, but many of his Muslim and Hindu coalition members[79] sensed that his star was waning. They increasingly saw that their long-term chances of office would be best served by severing their connections with Nazimuddin. The end came on 28 March when 21 members of the government voted against its budget proposals which were defeated by 106 votes to 97. The House was adjourned the next day by the Speaker, and Bengal entered an extended period of Governor's Rule which was to continue until the 1946 Provincial Elections.

THE 1946 ELECTIONS

The calling of elections in Bengal early in 1946 sparked off a scramble for League tickets between Nazimuddin and Suhrawardy's followers. Unlike in Sind, the League's more 'progressive' wing triumphed. Moreover, Abul Hashim's efforts ensured that the League could rely on local branches[80] to mobilize support, as well as turning to the traditional influence of *zamindars* and *Pirs*. The League had been further strengthened by the entry into its ranks of many Krishak Praja Party activists. Not surprisingly it swept to an overwhelming victory in Bengal which overshadowed its performance in the other 'Pakistan' areas.

Nazimuddin and Suhrawardy both had their eyes on the prize of the Chief Ministership after the elections. They, therefore, jockeyed for a dominant position in the process of selecting League candidates who would, of course, be loyal to them. Their enemies were to be left outside in the cold. The attempt to prevent Abul Hashim from getting a League ticket, by arranging for his rivals in the Burdwan District League to pass a no-confidence motion against him, was typical of the intrigue and infighting which went on.[81] The decision against Hashim was finally only overturned by a joint meeting of the Working Committee and Parliamentary Board. Such 'Party faction spirit' at a time when 'a life and death question' was about to be decided, caused much heart burning among some Bengal officials.[82] The Bengal League Working Committee attempted to damp down the rivalries by suspending all local League elections until the Provincial elections had been held.[83] Feelings were running so high, however, that ugly scenes occurred at the Provincial League Council Meeting which met on 29 September to form a Parliamentary Board.[84] Suhrawardy secured a majority of his followers on the Board.[85] He tightened still further his grip on the Bengal League by immediately dissolving the Election Fund and Provincial Propaganda Committees which had been created by the League's Working Committee and had a large contingent of Nazimuddin's supporters on them.[86] Henceforth, the League election campaign in Bengal was a one-man show. A group of Nazimuddin's supporters led by the Nawab of Dacca took their revenge by standing against the official League candidates.[87] This revolt was not as embarrassing as it might have been because the League's ranks had been greatly strengthened by an influx of Praja Party activists during the months before the elections.

By the beginning of 1946 the Krishak Praja Party had lost a large number of its members to the Muslim League. These included ex-Assembly members such as Ghyassuddin Ahmad, Nawabzada Syed Hasan Ali, Shamsuddin Ahmed, and a number of its high ranking officials. Such men as Nurul Islam (ex-Secretary Nikhil Banga Krishak Praja Samity) and Maqsud Ali Khan (ex-member of the Executive Committee of the

Nikhil Banga Krishak Praja Samity).[88] A number of non-Party men[89] also joined the Muslim League at this juncture. This influx into its ranks was part of a wider movement away from the regional Muslim parties[90] in the months which followed the Simla Conference. Jinnah's successful stand at the Conference, that every Muslim on the future Executive Council (in effect Interim Government) had to be a Leaguer, made it clear that India's future constitution would be decided by the two major parties, the Muslim League and the Congress, not by the regional parties. Their day was over.

Despite the intrigues which accompanied it, the League's election campaign in Bengal evoked scenes of unparalleled enthusiasm. It was inaugurated at a meeting held in Calcutta which was attended by half a million people.[91] Large crowds listened to the touring party of League propagandists in the Jalpaiguri District of north Bengal,[92] whilst a ten thousand-strong, mile-long procession of supporters bore Suhrawardy and his entourage into the town of Comilla in the easternmost part of Bengal.[93] The dark side of this popular outpouring of support for the Muslim League was the increasing violence with which its supporters broke up the opponents' meetings.[94] The League's Muslim rivals had come together to form the National Muslim Parliamentary Board. Its members soon found it impossible to hold a meeting without it being disrupted. Such violence and intimidation was an ominous sign for the future.

Pirs played a leading role in popularizing the League's message in Bengal as elsewhere in India. They were active local[95] and provincial members of the pro-League *Jamiat-ul-ulema-i-Islam*. The important *Urs* (death anniversary) ceremonies of leading shrines were used to drum up support for the Muslim League.[96] The *Pir* of Furfura addressed an open appeal to Fazlul Huq to come back into the Muslim fold and end his quarrel with the League leaders.[97] The *Pir* also exhorted his disciples to exert all their influence 'for the success of Muslim League candidates'.[98]

Students also flocked to the League's colours. They were trained in the art of mass contact at special camps in Calcutta and Dacca. The constituencies of the League's most prominent opponents, Fazlul Huq and Syed Nausher Ali, were especially targeted for their activities. Three hundred students worked in these constituencies, alone,[99] whilst throughout the province over seven and a half thousand students campaigned for the League.[100]

Jinnah's visit, late in February, climaxed the League's campaign. The Quaid-i-Azam addressed a mammoth meeting on 24 February. He hammered home the twin message that the Muslim League stood for the downtrodden and not the rich, and that it was fighting the elections not to capture ministries, but to create Pakistan.[101] By no means all of his followers in Bengal, however, shared these fine sentiments.

The League swept aside its rivals in the elections. It won 115 of the Muslim seats, receiving 95 per cent of the urban Muslim vote and 84 per cent of the rural vote. Prominent opponents such as Syed Nausher Ali and Nawab Habibullah of Dacca were decisively defeated. Fazlul Huq alone was able to withstand the League's victory tide. 'It may be fairly claimed by Mr. Jinnah', the new Governor, Frederick Burrows, reported, 'that the results show 2,013,000 votes polled for Pakistan and only 232,134 ... against'.[102] Burrows' arithmetic, however, simplified a far more complex situation.

THE PRELUDE TO PARTITION

Many Bengal Leaguers had campaigned in 1941 with the ideal of creating 'Purba-Pakistan', an independent, sovereign state consisting of the whole of Bengal and Assam. Jinnah's deliberate vagueness over the Pakistan Scheme and the ambiguous wording of the *1940 Lahore Resolution*[103] had allowed this idea to take root. The collapse of the *Cabinet Mission Plan* and the Great Calcutta Killing of 16 August ended all hopes of 'Purba-Pakistan', and made partition of Bengal itself a

serious reality. The Bengal League split into divisionists and
unionists. The former group of Eastern-Bengali Muslims were
happy to see partition. Mr. Abdul Ghufran, Minister of Civil
Supplies, stated openly that the loss of Calcutta would be
'good riddance', as it was 'a white elephant which produced
no food, but consumed huge amounts of foodstuffs'. Noorul
Amin, the Speaker of the Bengal Assembly, supported partition as he was confident it would bring him the Premiership
of East Bengal. He weaned Hamidah Haque Chaudhury away
from support for Greater Bengal Schemes by promising a
place in his Cabinet. Maulana Akram Khan wanted to retain
Calcutta for Pakistan, but was prepared to sacrifice the
Burdwan Division home of Abul Hashim.[104] The Unionists,
led by Suhrawardy, wanted to prevent partition at all costs.[105]
They included in their ranks Calcutta District Muslim League
Members, Kidderpore District Muslim League Members,
representatives of the Bihar Refugees Union, and the Asansul
Subdivision Muslim League. Suhrawardy worked hard
throughout May 1947 to bring about a united, independent
Bengal. He secured the support of the Congressmen, Surat
Bose and Kiran Shankar Roy, for this idea.[106] But the Congress High Command steadfastly backed the Hindu Mahas-
abha's demand for Partition. It chided Bose and Roy for their
unauthorized negotiations. The door was finally slammed on
Suhrawardy's proposals on 27 May when Nehru formally
announced that the Congress would only agree to a United
Bengal if it remained within the Indian Union.

The Partition of Bengal was a bitter blow to the expectations of many of its Muslim population. Whilst India inherited Calcutta, the City of Palaces, East Pakistan was endowed
with Dacca, city of bamboo and corrugated iron. The economic loss was even greater, however, than any cultural depri-
vation, for Calcutta contained the region's only modern port
and jute milling installations.[107] East Pakistan's problems
arising from industrial backwardness and poor communications were exacerbated by the thousand miles of Indian

territory which separated it from West Pakistan. Moreover, the new balance of power in the East Pakistan Muslim League did not augur well for a solution of these difficulties. The conservative Dacca old guard re-established itself, as Partition robbed both Suhrawardy and Abul Hashim of their power-base. Nazimuddin once more became Prime Minister, reversing the decline in the aristocracy's position. The Bengali speaking Praja activists who had done so much to build a mass base for the League in 1944-7 now found that Pakistan meant the rule of the landowning Urdu minority.

REFERENCE

1. Although it must be remembered that the bulk of the Muslims even in Mughal times were lowly cultivators.
2. Hindu cultivators also suffered from the effects of the Permanent Settlement, but as more Muslims were cultivators, they suffered disproportionately.
3. Landlords took advantage of the situation by illegally raising rents.
4. Many of the hereditary Hindu *zamindars* had lost their holdings to profess-ional *'bhadralok'* high caste families, of Brahmins and Kayasthas.
5. Chatterjee, P., 'Bengal Politics and the Muslim Masses, 1920-47', in *The Journal of Commonwealth and Comparative Politics*, XX, March 1982, p. 31.
6. *Bengal District Administration Committee Report 1913-14*, Calcutta, 1915, p. 176.
7. The educational pioneers were Nawab Abdul Latif (1828-93) and Syed Ameer Ali (1849-1928).
8. This was founded in 1921.
9. These were Nazimuddin (the Chief Minister) and his younger brother Shahabuddin.
10. Such men as Haji Adamji Daud and M.A.H. Ispahani.
11. There was, in fact, a specifically Muslim Bengali literature. Moreover, Bengali Muslims spoke their native tongue with a mixture of Urdu and Persian words.
12. Hussain Shaheed Suhrawardy rose to power as the organizer of this labour force.
13. Hajji Shariat Allah (1781-1840) launched a movement calling on Muslims to observe strictly the duties (*faraiz* hence the name of *Faraizi* given to the Movement) enjoined by the Qur'an. It gained large numbers of adherents in the districts of Faridpur, Bakarganj, Dacca, and Mymensingh under the leadership of Hajji Shariat Allah's son. The Movement intermixed religious enthusiasm with militant opposition to the economic oppression of Hindu landlords and moneylenders. Titu Mir's movement in West Bengal similarly linked religious reform with social and political militancy.
14. For forty years he led a travelling college of reformers up and down the river systems of East Bengal. The *Faraizi* Movement had attacked the reverencing of *Pirs,* Maulana Karamat Ali Jaunpuri opposed this, although he advocated reform of some Sufi practices.
15. The Hindu renaissance of the second half of the nineteenth century was a further factor in widening the gulf between the communities.
16. This was itself a new party formed only in May 1936.
17. The League as a result found itself in the unusual position of having better funding and newspaper support than its rivals.

18. The League thus had a foothold, unlike elsewhere, in the politically important rural areas. Although its best performance was in the urban constituencies, it did win 29 rural seats and capture 26 per cent of the rural Muslim votes.
19. Huq had formed this Party in April 1936 after he had captured, with radical East Bengal support, its predecessor, the Nikhil Banga Praja Samity (All-Bengal Tenants' Association).
20. The Praja Party did lay itself open to charges that it was un-Islamic by its informal electoral arrangement with the Congress.
21. *Star of India*, 11 December 1936.
22. *Star of India*, 22 and 23 December 1936.
23. This was a very different situation to Jinnah's relations with the Punjab Premier Sikander. See Chapter 4.
24. He had earlier unsuccessfully negotiated with the Congress.
25. Huq's Praja Party colleague was the Minister of Public Health and Local Self Government, Syed Nausher Ali. The Muslim League Ministers were Khawaja Nazimuddin, Nawab Habibullah, Nawab Musharraff Hosain, and H.S. Suhrawardy.
26. Bengal FR, first half of June and first half of August 1937, L/P&J/5/141 IOR.
27. Bengal FR, second half of September 1937, L/P&J/5/141 IOR.
28. The Acts' passing into Law was publicly celebrated on 28 August 1938. Bengal FR, second half of August 1938, L/P&J/5/143 IOR.
29. For full details of the measure see *A Resume of the Bengal Government's Activities Since April 1937*, Alipore, 1938, p. 1 and ff.
30. Brabourne to Linlithgow, 5 May 1938, L/P&J/5/146 IOR.
31. Bengal FR, 22 April 1940, L/P&J/5/146 IOR.
32. The League's Working Committee had asked Party members not to serve on the War Committees. Nazimuddin supported Huq's decision to disobey this, although Ispahani backed the Party line.
33. Bengal FR, second half of September, first half of October 1941, L/P&J/5/148 IOR.
34. FR for the second half of December 1937, L/P&J/5/141 IOR.
35. FR for the first half of February 1938, L/P&J/5/142 IOR.
36. FR for the first half of May 1938, L/P&J/5/142 IOR.
37. *Star of India*, 14 February 1942.
38. Mookerji resigned on 20 November 1942, claiming that the Governor and British officials were exercising undue influence on the Chief Minister. Huq struggled on in office for another year.
39. Herbert to Linlithgow, 11 February 1942, L/P&J/5/149 IOR.
40. *Star of India*, 23 January 1942.
41. Raghib Ahsan to Jinnah, 15 November 1944, SHC Sind Vol. 4:18.
42. Bengal FR, 21 April 1942, L/P&J/5/149 IOR.
43. Bengal had, of course, faced a real threat of Japanese invasion in the spring of 1942, FR, second half of March 1943, L/P&J/5/150.
44. Suhrawardy had failed in two attempts to wrest the leadership of the Muslim League Assembly Party out of Nazimuddin's hands. Suhrawardy's greatest support came from the party organization, although he had to give up the post of Secretary in 1943.
45. A major plank almost inevitably was the abolition of *zamindari* landlordism and the Permanent Settlement. Hashim also called for the nationalization of the jute industry. Sen, S., *Muslim Politics in Bengal 1937-47*, New Delhi, 1976, p. 184.
46. League propaganda in Punjab followed a similar line. See Chapter 4.
47. It was India's first famine since the *Famine Code* was devised in 1883.
48. This was clogged by the mounting allied war efforts. In eastern coastal districts the 'denial' policy in the face of a Japanese invasion threat had led to boats and bridges being destroyed, thus making it difficult to move food stocks around.

49. Moon, P. (editor), *Wavell—The Viceroy's Journal*, London, 1973, p. 56.
50. Rutherford to Wavell, 17/23 November 1943, L/P&J/5/150 IOR.
51. Herbert to Linlithgow, 28 August 1943, L/P&J/5/150 IOR.
52. He had the unenviable job of Food Minister.
53. Bengal FR, 10 January 1944, L/P&J/5/151 IOR.
54. Bengal FR, first half of August 1943, L/P&J/5/151 IOR.
55. Sen, op. cit., 1976, p. 175. This ruling principally affected Suhrawardy who was both Minister for Food and Bengal League Secretary at the time.
56. The Party President, Maulana Akram Khan, supported the Nazimuddin faction, but he was little more than a figurehead.
57. Bengal was entitled to send 100 members to the 465-strong Council. Jalal, op. cit., 1985, pp. 40, 103.
58. Raghib Ahsan to Jinnah, 15 November 1944, SHC Bengal 4:18.
59. Ibid.
60. Review of the Muslim League Organization in Bengal submitted by Secretary, Bengal Provincial Muslim League to Secretary, All-India Muslim League, 30 July 1944, SHC Bengal 1:42.
61. Ibid.
62. Ibid.
63. Raghib Ahsan to Jinnah, 17 November 1944, SHC Bengal 4:19.
64. Tippera had 52,000 members, Barisal 160,000. Raghib Ahsan to Jinnah, 15 November 1944, SHC Bengal 4:18.
65. Abdul Hashim to Jinnah, 25 November 1944, SHC Bengal 1:43.
66. Raghib Ahsan to Jinnah, 15 November 1944, SHC Bengal 4:18.
67. Abdul Hashim to Jinnah, 25 November 1944, SHC Bengal 1:43.
68. Syed Muezemuddin Husain helped enroll members in the Mymensingh District.
69. Raghib Ahsan assured Jinnah that Hashim was a 'Rabbani' or a Muslim believing in the ideology and social economy of Islamic Rabubiat as preached by the Qur'an and Sunnah. Raghib Ahsan to Jinnah, 15 November 1944, SHC Bengal 4:18.
70. Review of the Muslim League Organization in Bengal submitted by Secretary, Bengal Provincial Muslim League to Secretary, All-India Muslim League, 30 July 1944, SHC Bengal 1:42.
71. Report of Abdul Hashim to the Annual Council Meeting of the Bengal Provincial Muslim League, November 1944. Bengal Provincial Muslim League 1944, Vol. 41, FMA. In this same report Hashim gave further information concerning District membership. He noted that the Mymensingh branch had 41,000 members, Chittagong 40,000, Noakhali 50,000, Dinajpur 24,500, Faridpur 60,000, Rangipur 13,470, and Murshidabad 2,000.
72. Raghib Ahsan to Jinnah, 17 November 1944, SHC Bengal 4:19.
73. Raghib Ahsan to Jinnah, 18 November 1944, SHC Bengal 4:20.
74. Raghib Ahsan to Jinnah, 19 November 1944, SHC Bengal 4:21.
75. Ibid. Suhrawardy promised Raghib Ahsan, the Working Committee Secretary, that he would see to it that the Prime Minister would 'work honestly and faithfully for the masses' and not 'align himself with toadies and reactionary job-hunters'.
76. Bengal FR for the second half of January 1945, L/P&J/5/152 IOR.
77. Bengal FR for the first half of March 1945, L/P&J/5/152 IOR.
78. President Bakarganj Muslim League to Jinnah, 19 December 1945, SHC Bengal 1:77.
79. It should be remembered that although this was a League Government in name, it contained six Hindu members.
80. Abul Hashim calculated that the League's membership in 1945 was around ten per cent of the Muslim population.
81. Bengal Provincial Muslim League, 1945, Part IX, Vol. 42, p. 91, FMA.
82. See for example Asadullah to Liaquat Ali Khan, 17 September 1945. Ibid., p. 48.

83. Resolution of the Working Committee of the Bengal Provincial Muslim League, 27 August 1945, Part IX, Vol. 42, p. 40.
84. Some members were actually injured. Jalal, op. cit., 1985, p. 155.
85. These were Abul Hashim, Ahmed Hussein, Raghib Ahsan, and Moazzem Hossein. Telegram to Liaquat Ali Khan, 1 October 1945. Bengal Provincial Muslim League 1945, Part IX, Vol. 42, p. 91, FMA.
86. The Parliamentary Board took over the Committees' responsibilities.
87. Twenty-six League members in all, including the Nawab of Dacca, were expelled.
88. *Star of India,* 9 January 1946.
89. Such men as Maulvi Mirza Abdul Hafiz, K.B. Muhammad Ali Khan, and Choudhury Zahur Ahmed.
90. See Chapter 4 for the example of this process in Punjab.
91. Suhrawardy to Jinnah, telegram, 28 December 1945, SHC Bengal 3:15.
92. *Star of India,* 22 December 1945.
93. *Star of India,* 30 November 1945.
94. Bengal FR for the second half of November 1945, L/P&J/5/152 IOR.
95. *Star of India,* 29 October 1945.
96. *Star of India,* 7 February 1946.
97. *Dawn,* 14 November 1945.
98. *Star of India,* 19 March 1946.
99. *Star of India,* 4 March 1946.
100. *Star of India,* 15 March 1946.
101. *Star of India,* 25 February 1946.
102. Bengal FR for the second half of March 1946, L/P&J/5/153 IOR.
103. Its third paragraph called for the grouping of contiguous Muslim majority areas in north-west and eastern India into 'Independent States in which the constituent units would be autonomous and sovereign'.
104. Memorandum to Jinnah from the Calcutta District Muslim League, 31 May 1947, QIAP F/104.
105. The Calcutta League claimed that with the support of the Muslim seamen and port workers, it could bring the docks to a standstill if the Hindus forcibly attempted to keep Calcutta in India.
106. The agreement included provisions for Joint Electorates, reservation of seats on population basis and an Inter-Communal Ministry. Sen, op. cit., 1976, p. 238 and ff.
107. The loss of the mills and workshops of Hooghly and Howrah together with the coal fields of the areas which bordered on Bihar, meant that although East Bengal contained two-thirds of the population of United Bengal, it inherited only 12 per cent of the industrial installations. Symons, R., *Making of Pakistan,* Karachi, 1986, p. 153.

The League-Unionist Conflict within Punjab

The Punjab was the most important of all the major centres of Muslim population to the Pakistan Scheme, because of its strategic geographical position, its large Muslim majority and its agricultural wealth. It formed the heartland of a future Pakistan State, Jinnah indeed called it the 'cornerstone of Pakistan'. If the Punjabi Muslims had not supported the Muslim League's separatist demand, Pakistan could never have come into existence. Yet the League was even more a latecomer in the Punjab than in the other Muslim majority areas. Unlike in Sind and the Frontier, it did not recover from a poor showing in the 1937 elections to form a wartime government. In fact, Punjab was the only 'Pakistan' area in which the League did not hold office before Partition. The reason for this was the Unionist Party's dominance in the Punjab countryside where all but 10 of the 85 Muslim constituencies were situated. It is first necessary to understand the roots of the Unionist Party's pre-eminence, before examining in detail the way in which the Muslim League was able to achieve its vital breakthrough in 1946-7.

THE HISTORICAL ROOTS OF
THE UNIONIST PREDOMINANCE

The Unionist Party was founded by Mian Fazl-i-Husain[1] and Chhotu Ram[2] in 1923. From that date until 1946 it dominated politics within Punjab. It functioned more as a loose coalition of Muslim, Hindu, and Sikh cultivators, than as a modern political party. It did not, for example, formally contest elections to the Legislative Council and in 1937 to the new Assembly. It was only after the rural members had entered the Legislature that they joined together to form a Unionist group. They had not been elected because of the popularity of their Party's programme, but because of their economic, social or religious influence over the voters. All the Unionist Council and Assembly members were substantial landowners who assisted the British district officials either as honorary magistrates or as *Zaildars*. The *Zaildars'* duty was to render general assistance to all government officials in the circle, or *Zail*, of usually ten to thirty villages under his control, to supervise the village headmen, and to act as an honorary police officer-in-charge of the village police. This post symbolized the importance which the British attached to the support of Punjabi landholders. The Unionist Party was the legacy of over half a century of such close ties.

Punjab's strategic situation and its emergence by the 1880s as the major recruiting area of the Indian Army led the British to make strenuous efforts to win the political support of the major landowning groups. In the eastern regions, these consisted of powerful *biraderis* of both Muslim and Hindu Jat peasant proprietors, while most of the land in the predominantly Muslim western half of the Punjab was owned by large landlords.[3] The latter were usually clan leaders or *pirs* who had considerable landholdings attached to their shrines.[4] The descendants of Baba Farid, the Punjab's leading Sufi saint, owned some 43,000 acres in all.[5] The shrine of his thirteenth century contemporary, Sheikh Baha'u'd-din Zakariya, an important saint of the Suhrawardi Sufi Order, owned 5,000 acres in Multan. The British adopted a variety of means to secure the loyalty of the rural powerholders. They pitched tax demands as low as practicable, dispensed patronage in the form of honorary ranks and titles, and gave them lucrative land grants in the fertile canal colony districts.[6]

The rapid rise of agricultural prices and land values which followed from the Pax Britannica and improved communications and irrigation, eventually threatened rural political stability. British rule had swept away the barriers that had previously prevented urban moneylenders from acquiring land in the countryside. As land prices rose, it became increasingly tempting for landowners to pledge their land in return for easy credit, and land began to pass into the money-lenders' hands at an alarming rate. The fear that this would result in widespread unrest led the British to take encumbered estates under the wing of the Court of Wards, which by 1895 was managing as many as 65 estates with a total area of 344,000 acres. The Court of Wards revitalized the estates under its control by the introduction of sound management techniques and improvements in irrigation, stock breeding, and cultivation. To deal more widely with the problem, the British introduced major legislation in 1901 to curb the moneylenders' influence. *The Punjab Alienation of Land Act* divided the population into agriculturalist and non-agriculturalist tribes, the latter including the main moneylending groups were forbidden to permanently acquire land in the countryside.

In the short term, the measure halted the expropriation of impoverished landowners. In the long term, it encouraged intercommunal political co-operation by its recognition of the rural Muslim, Hindu, and Sikh communities' common interests. These were further boosted by the creation of the Punjab Legislative Council in 1897 which was dominated by the landowning groups. The first rural intercommunal political association within Punjab was formed in 1907 by Sardar Partap Singh Alhuwalia, and was called the Association of the Landed Aristocracy of the Punjab, later renamed the Punjab Chief's Association. As its name implies, it was an intensely conservative and loyalist organization, serving the landowners and the British interests equally well by limiting Congress's influence and preventing infection of the countryside with the communal tensions which had dominated political life in Punjabi towns from the 1880s onwards.

The British success in winning the support of rural allies was clearly demonstrated when the Punjab was subjected to the strains and stresses of the First World War. The landowners not only assisted in raising large numbers of recruits for the Indian Army, but helped limit the impact of both the revolutionary Sikh Ghadr Movement[7] and the Khilafat agitation. The disturbances in 1919 that resulted in the infamous Jallianwala Bagh massacre in Amritsar were, in fact, limited to only a handful of the province's towns. The Deputy Commissioner of the Gujrat District reported that the villagers in his area had not even heard of the agitation against the *Rowlatt Act*.[8]

The landowners' ties with the British grew even closer following the passage of the *Montagu-Chelmsford Reforms* in 1919, which increased the franchise and transferred control of certain subjects of provincial administration, such as education and local self-government, to ministers responsible to a new Legislative Council. The most important aspect of the reforms from the Punjab's viewpoint was the institutional-ization of the existing political divisions between rural and urban political interests. Separate electorates were created for the Punjab's towns and countryside, and only members of the agricultural tribes, as defined by the *Alienation of Land Act, 1901* were allowed to stand as candidates for the rural constituencies. This paved the way for the creation of the Unionist Party in 1923.

The Unionist Party's success depended on a careful bal-ancing of the interests of its Muslim landlord and Hindu Jat wings. The British bent over backwards to make this possible. A striking example of the benefits which could be obtained by united action was given to the rural population in 1924, when the Punjab Government considerably reduced the enhancement of the canal water rates after widespread protests, even though this meant that it had to rearrange the provincial budget and reintroduce urban taxation. Another British concession to joint action was the *Land Revenue Act, 1928* which, with its lighter assessments and the fixing of 40 years as the period of settlement, benefited both the landlords and peasant proprietors.

Although the Unionist Party lost some of its power when Mian Fazl-i-Husain left the Punjab in 1930 to take up his position on the Viceroy's Executive Council, it nevertheless exerted a dominant and moderating influence on provincial politics throughout the period 1923-37. The Unionists also extended their influence into All-India Muslim politics in the late 1920s. Mohammad Shafi[9] and Mian Fazl-i-Husain created the All-India Muslim Conference to represent the majority areas' interests in such issues as opposition to joint electorates,[10] and co-operation with the Simon Commission. The Unionist controlled All-India Muslim Conference eclipsed the All-India Muslim League in the early 1930s, making it impossible for the League's Punjab branch to overturn the Unionist Party's position.

The Punjab officials, as they had done earlier in 1919, ensured that the constitutional reforms of the *Government of India Act, 1935* did not weaken the position of their rural allies. Only a quarter of the new electorate of 2.75 million voters consisted of members of the non-agriculturalist tribes. All landowners who paid Rs. 5 and upwards in Land Revenue were enfranchised, as were tenants who occupied more than six acres of irrigated land, or 12 acres of unirrigated land. The Muslim League thus faced a major problem in 1937. It had to somehow undermine the Unionist Party's entrenched position in the countryside, if it was to make any impact in the region during the new era of Provincial Autonomy.

THE 1937 PUNJAB ELECTIONS

Jinnah attempted to bring existing Punjabi political groupings under the wing of the Muslim League Parliamentary Board in May 1936. Mian Fazl-i-Husain, however, rejected these overtures, sending Jinnah empty-handed and embittered from Lahore.[11] Thereafter, the League was doomed to almost certain defeat. The composition of its touring Propaganda Committee highlighted the difficulties which it faced in mobilizing support in the countryside. There was only one landowner amongst its 15 members, seven of whom were lawyers or urban politicians from Lahore. The policies which they advocated had little appeal for the rural population. The only response which the League could make to the *pirs'* support for the Unionist Party[12] was to issue an appeal to the Punjabi Muslims exhorting them in the name of Islam to vote for candidates of the Muslim League Parliamentary Board.[13] The fact that it was issued in Urdu, the language of the educated townsmen, rather than Punjabi, revealed the limited extent of the League's appeal to the rural population at that time. Its influence was so limited that it encountered great difficulty in finding candidates who were willing to oppose the Unionists. A derisory eight candidates finally fought under its banner. Although the situation might still have been retrieved if the League had made overtures to the large number of Independents.

As soon as the first results were announced on 1 February 1937, it was clear that the Unionists had secured a great victory. This was confirmed when the non-Party candidates announced their allegiance to the Unionist Assembly Party. At the final count, the Unionists had captured 99 of the 175 seats. The Muslim League had managed just two. The Unionist supremacy in the countryside was confirmed. The Party had won 73 of the 75 rural Muslim seats and all but one of the rural Hindu seats in the Jat heartland of the Ambala Division. Rural voters continued to be as influenced by the landlords and *pirs* as in earlier Legislative Council elections.

The Unionist Party's victory created a major problem for the Muslim League. It had to undermine its predominance, if Jinnah's claim to be the sole representative of Indian Muslims was not to sound embarrassingly hollow and his bargaining position in All-India politics be seriously weakened. This became even more imperative after the *Lahore Resolution* was passed in 1940 and the heartland of Pakistan remained under Unionist domination. In order to challenge the Unionist

Party's position, the League had somehow to extend its influence from the towns into the villages. These attempts took three main stages. In the first, which began soon after the elections and was brought to an abrupt halt by the Pact between Sikander,[14] the Unionist Premier, and Jinnah in October 1937, the League attempted to build a mass organizational base in the countryside. In the second, which lasted from 1937 until the collapse of the Jinnah-Khizr Talks in April 1944, the League was effectively under Unionist control, and had to rely on the efforts of the Punjab Muslim Students' Federation and on urban religious leaders to popularize its demand for Pakistan amongst the rural voters. Towards the end of this period, it also tried to win support by exploiting wartime discontent. The final phase, which really began in earnest only after the collapse of the Simla Conference in August 1945, saw an intensification of the process of attacking the Unionists for wartime dislocation. At the same time, the League made a major effort to win over the support of the leading landlords and *pirs*. This strategy enabled it to turn the tables on the Unionist Party in the 1946 elections. It still took, however, a campaign of direct action similar to that in the Frontier, to finally unseat the Unionists in March 1947. Before turning to the last and most vital period of the League's development in the province, we shall briefly examine its earlier, abortive efforts to expand into the countryside.

THE PERIOD OF UNIONIST ASCENDANCY 1937-40

The Punjab Muslim League emerged from its drubbing in the 1937 elections, determined to build a mass base of support in the countryside. During the summer months, it launched a vigorous rural propaganda campaign. Workers were sent into the villages to form primary League branches,[15] and the membership fee was reduced to only four *annas* to encourage as many villagers as possible to join. The Punjab League hoped to enrol at this time as many as 20,000 new primary members in the Lahore district alone.[16] A number of Provincial League leaders toured the rural areas to whip up enthusiasm for this membership drive. In September, Malik Zeman Mehdi Khan, the Deputy President, and Ghulam Rasul, the Honorary Secretary, toured Gujranwala and established a district branch of the League there and encouraged the formation of primary branches in the villages.[17] The success of the Unionist ministry's agrarian reforms,[18] however, meant that the Muslim League faced an uphill struggle. Its faltering efforts were brought to an end, by the Pact which was signed between Jinnah and Sikander at the October 1937 Lucknow Session of the All-India Muslim League. Under its terms, Sikander agreed to advise all the Muslim members of the Unionist Party to join the Muslim League. They would form a Punjab Muslim League Assembly Party which would be subject to the rules and regulations of the Central and Provincial Parliamentary Boards of the League. The agreement was not, however, to affect the continuation of the Ministry, which would still be given its Unionist Party name.

The reason why Sikander agreed to the Pact and what its authors precisely meant still remains controversial. M.A.H. Ispahani has depicted Sikander as joining the Muslim League not out of deep conviction, but merely as a matter of necessity, in order to strengthen his ministry in the face of the threat from the Congress Mass Contact Movement which was launched in Punjab in April 1937.[19] This grossly exaggerates, however, both that threat and the Muslim League's influence in the province. Sajjad Zaheer and Ashiq Hussain Batalvi on the other hand have criticized Sikander for agreeing to the Pact solely with the intention of gobbling up the Punjab Muslim League organization.[20] Even its Punjabi co-drafters, Sikander and Malik Barkat Ali, completely contradicted each other's interpretations of its political consequences for the region.[21]

There is no denying, however, that the Pact's immediate effect was greatly to strengthen the Muslim League's position in All-India politics.[22] But Sikander lost nothing by this move. For whilst the All-India Muslim League's position was revitalized, he assumed complete control of the Punjab Muslim League. Sikander only acquiesced to the Pact on the understanding that the Punjab Muslim League would be reorganized afterwards.[23] This wish was granted in March 1938 when it was refused reaffiliation to the All-India League on the controversial grounds that its constitution was irregular.[24] At the April 1938 Calcutta Muslim League Session, an Organizing Committee was formed under Sikander's chairmanship with the task of creating a new Muslim League organization within the province.[25] The following month the old Punjab Muslim League was dissolved. Sikander, despite Malik Barkat Ali's protests, ensured that Unionists were in the majority on the Organizing Committee. Only 10 of its 35 members were 'old' Muslim Leaguers. The Organizing Committee delayed for so long that it was finally given the deadline of 15 November 1939 by which date to establish a new Punjab League. Just a week before this ran out, it announced the formation of a new provincial organization. Two more months passed before its inaugural meeting was held. Significantly, this took place under Sikander's chairmanship at his Lahore residence. Predictably, all the officials who were elected at this meeting were loyal Unionists. The Muslim League's genuine supporters violently protested. A number of district officials resigned. The Montgomery District League wrote directly to Jinnah asking him to take action.[26] The widespread protests finally forced the All-India leadership to send a Committee of Enquiry in February 1939. After a few days' stay, it recommended that the Punjab League's affiliation be accepted. This decision was a tremendous triumph for Sikander. It marked the zenith of the Unionist Party's power within the Punjab.

Malik Barkat Ali and his supporters were incredulous that Jinnah should have allowed the Unionist Party to gain complete control of their organization.[27] They failed to realize how heavily Jinnah depended on Sikander's support as a

result of the All-India Muslim League's poor showing in the
Indian Provincial Elections. Throughout the years 1937-40
the League's prestige was greatly enhanced by the support
which it received from the Punjab's powerful Premier. Moreover, Sikander on such occasions as the December 1938
Patna Muslim League Session enabled Jinnah to overcome the
opposition of the radicals within his own organization.[28] In
return, he made sure that Barkat Ali's resolution calling for
the immediate dissolution of the Organizing Committee was
thrown out. Jinnah could ill afford to displease Sikander
whose assistance was as useful in internal League politics as in
dealings with the Congress and the British. The price he had
to pay for this was the virtual halt of all the League's organizational activities in the Punjab countryside. These did not
begin again in earnest until the Second World War transformed
Jinnah's status and enabled him to dispense with Unionist
backing.

THE PUNJAB MUSLIM LEAGUE 1940-4

Under the Unionists' control, the Muslim League's rural
development ground to a complete halt. The seven city and
six district branches of the League which returned membership
figures in 1941 showed a total number of just under 15,000
persons enrolled. In ten districts there was no local League
organization at all.[29]

The little propaganda that was carried out, was the work
of the Punjab Muslim Students' Federation. It had been
reorganized in 1937 by Abdul Sattar Khan Niazi, Ibrahim Ali
Chishti, and Hameed Nizami. The majority of its members
came from Islamia College, Lahore. The Federation strongly
supported the demand for Pakistan and organized a Pakistan
Conference at Lahore in March 1941, at which Jinnah presided. At this Conference, a Pakistan Rural Propaganda Committee was created with Nizami as its Secretary. Towards the
end of May he wrote fervently to Jinnah, 'We have fully

determined', he declared, 'that to win the land of Pakistan, we will launch one attack after another like Ghaznavi ... For a long time the saints of Somnath[30] have been waiting for another like him'.[31] During the course of a 20-day tour of Sheikhupura, the Committee visited 50 villages in each of which it opened a primary branch of the Muslim League.[32] Although this represented only a tiny drop in the ocean, it was a useful dress rehearsal for the students' propaganda campaigns in the countryside during the 1946 elections.

Table 4.1: The Punjab Muslim League's Primary Membership Figures for 1941

Name of District	Number of Primary Members	Number of Primary Leagues
1. Montgomery City	227	—
2. Amritsar	765	22
3. Batala City	300	1
4. Montgomery	3200	20
5. Sheikhupura	500	36
6. Sialkot	1500	15
7. Rawalpindi City	1200	8
8. Attock	491	6
9. Ferozepore City	255	6
10. Rohtak City	250	3
11. Ferozepore	3515	15
12. Rewari City	620	1
13. Lahore City	2000	5
Total	14823	138

Source: Conference of the Presidents and Secretaries of the Provincial Muslim Leagues, October 1941, Vol. 326, Part 2, p. 74, FMA.

By the beginning of 1943, the Unionists' stock was falling because of wartime discontent, whilst the All-India Muslim League's status was rising. The Punjab Muslim League began to tentatively resume its official activities in the countryside. Eight new primary Leagues were established in January and

February and conferences were held at Fazilka, Karwal, Amritsar, and Chiniot.[33] These efforts were not enough, however, to satisfy a group of local activists who formed a Muslim League Workers' Board under the chairmanship of Nawabzada Rashid Ali Khan, President of the Lahore Muslim League. The Workers' Board aimed to establish new District and Primary Leagues and to revitalize those which already existed so that half a million 2-annas members could be enrolled in the Punjab. This unauthorized action was condemned by the Punjab League officials,[34] although Rashid Ali Khan strenuously denied their accusation that the Workers' Board was a rival to the Provincial branch of the Muslim League. Jinnah demonstrated his growing authority in Punjabi affairs, when he forced Rashid Ali Khan to wind up the Workers' Board early in March. The Nawabzada continued to complain, however, about the League President. 'How could the Punjab League grow', he asked, 'if its leader (the Nawab of Mamdot) refused to allow Primary League branches to be established on his Ferozepore estate?'[35] Jinnah ignored his complaints, as he did those about Nizamuddin in Bengal and Hidayatullah in Sind. He nevertheless determined to remove the ambiguities caused by his Pact with Sikander.

THE UNIONIST PARTY IN DECLINE

The new Unionist Premier, Khizr Hayat Khan Tiwana, who succeeded Sikander[36] early in 1943, found himself in an increasingly difficult situation. The wartime policies of heavy army recruitment and the requisitioning and rationing of foodgrains undermined the Unionist Party's popularity in the countryside whilst in the Assembly Khizr faced the threat of increasing factional rivalries amongst the landowners.[37] Jinnah took advantage of these problems to force Khizr's hand. Early in April 1944, he had talks with Khizr endeavouring to clarify the relationship between the Unionist Party and the League in Punjabi politics. A compromise formula was drafted and discussed, but the talks finally broke down over Khizr's insistence that the new coalition ministry which would be created after the establishment of a Muslim League Assembly Party should return the Unionist Party name. A bitter dispute followed in which the League denied that it had ever recognized the Jinnah-Sikander Talks of 1937 as constituting a formal and a binding Pact. It culminated with Khizr's expulsion from the Muslim League in May. Within six months, the Muslim League Assembly Party stood at 27 members. These included representatives of such leading landlord families as the Noons, Daultanas, and Hayats, from which the Unionist Party had traditionally drawn its leadership.[38]

The Muslim League stepped up its rural propaganda in the wake of the collapse of the Jinnah-Khizr Talks. Student workers toured the villages exploiting the growing wartime discontent.[39] They took medical supplies with them which had become increasingly difficult to obtain. They also distributed cloth and endeavoured to obtain increased ration allowances for the villagers.[40] Most of all they linked the solution of the peasants' economic and social problems with the successful establishment of a Pakistan state, in a manner reminiscent of Abul Hashim's workers in Bengal. The Punjab League also attempted to crystallize rural opposition[41] to the requisitioning of grain supplies which had been forced on the Unionist Party by the Central Food Department.[42] It also expressed the increasing dissatisfaction with the Unionist Party's failure to control inflation and curb the profiteering of Hindu and Sikh businessmen.[43] The alleged communal bias of Hindu and Sikh Civil Supply Officers formed another powerful theme in Muslim League propaganda. In May 1945, for example, the League held a series of protest meetings in the leading mosques of Lahore to complain about the way cloth was distributed in the city.[44]

The Muslim League's fresh landlord converts, Mian Mumtaz Daultana and Shaukat Hayat, played an important role in taking the Pakistan message to the countryside in the summer of 1944. During June and July they toured all five of the

Province's Divisions and addressed Muslim League Conferences
at Montgomery, Lyallpur, Sheikhupura, Sargodha, Jhang,
Sialkot, and Rawalpindi. These attracted large audiences,
over 15,000 attended the meeting at Multan and 10,000 at
Montgomery.[45] For the first time ever, primary League
branches were established in such rural areas as Sargodha and
Mianwali. In July alone it was reported that 7,000 members
had been enrolled in these two areas.

Despite this advance, the Unionist Party's grip on the
countryside could not be broken overnight. It still continued
to win District Board and Provincial Assembly bye-elections
throughout 1944. In August, for example, it defeated the
Muslim League in the Sialkot District Board elections.[46]
Unionist candidates were also returned for the Hoshiarpur
and Kanara and Jhajjar Legislative Assembly seats. The
League's organizational advance was also slow. As late as May
1945 it could still only boast of a Punjab membership of
150,000.[47] Local factional rivalries were undoubtedly imped-
ing its advance. In the Gujjar Khan and Rawalpindi Districts,
these were so acute that parallel Leagues competed against
each other.[48] More important, however, was the landowners'
grip over the rural population. The large *zamindars* obstructed
League activists who they saw a disruptive to their lucrative
connection with the British. There was a heavy and intimidat-
ing police presence at many rural Muslim League gatherings.
'The Punjab is the darling of the bureaucrats', Mian Mumtaz
Daultana explained to Jinnah in June 1945, 'The people of
the Punjab have never known political consciousness, are
untrained to modern political ways of thought, have never
experienced organized political effort ... For a nation to
shake off the cobwebs of time takes time. In two to three
years I can promise you a fully conscious and determined
Muslim Punjab'.[49] The Muslim League did not have that long,
however, to establish a mass organization in Punjab. The key
to its success in the vital 1946 Provincial Elections thus hinged
on the support it could obtain from the rural elite.[50]

By the end of 1945, there had been a large scale defection from the Unionist Party to the Muslim League. The Punjab League like its counterparts elsewhere in Muslim India welcomed late converts with open arms, as they commanded influence over the rural voters. Some 'conversions' were genuine and at the personal cost of risking official displeasure. Many, however, were opportunistic in response to mounting pressures from below,[51] and the League's new authority at the Centre.

The transformation of the Muslim League's status during the Second World War together with the British decision to leave India demoralized their landlord allies in the Unionist Party. A growing number came to believe that in the light of these new circumstances, Unionism had outlived its *raison d'etre*. Khizr himself shared many of the rural elite's misgivings about future political developments. He repeatedly expressed the fear that the British would let down their allies and that he and his supporters would suffer for opposing the Muslim League.[52] He aired the intention of retiring to his estate at the end of the war, and made it plain that he was only remaining in office to serve the war effort. In order to protect himself from future recriminations he pleaded with the Punjab Governor to give him an official 'order' to stand up to Jinnah in the interests of the war effort. Sir Bertrand Glancy naturally rejected this appeal, although he was forced to admit that 'there is a good deal of force in Khizr's apprehension'.[53]

As the Muslim League's influence grew in national politics, first with the Viceroy's August 1940 Declaration and later with the *Cripps Mission's* acceptance of separatist demands,[54] its attitude hardened towards the Unionist Party. Khizr was branded as a traitor. At the local level, the Muslim League stirred up trouble amongst the tenants of Unionist landlords. The Rajpur Assembly members for the Rawalpindi East and Gujjar Khan constituencies, Major Farman Ali and Raja Fateh Khan, both joined the League's ranks as a result of such pressure.[55]

After the collapse of the Simla Conference in July 1945, there was even greater strain on the loyalty of Unionist supporters. The Conference brought home the fact that the receipt of high office in future would depend on collaboration with the Muslim League rather than the British. It was this new awareness, rather than the League's renewed depiction of Khizr as a traitor to Islam, which sparked off the rural elite's large-scale exodus from the Unionist Party during the weeks which followed the Simla Conference. It had been looked to for patronage and to safeguard the landowners' local interests. When it became uncertain whether it would be able to continue to discharge these functions, they deserted it. Khizr was even abandoned by his kinsmen, Firoz Khan Noon, Malik Sardar Noon, and Major Mohammad Mumtaz Khan Tiwana. He was left to reflect bitterly how the Viceroy had let him down by his handling of Jinnah at Simla.[56] The months after Simla also witnessed a strengthening of the League's position in Bengal and the Frontier. But nowhere else was it as dramatic and decisive as in Punjab.

The League was also boosted by the entry of a large number of Punjabi *Pirs* during the years 1944-6. As early as April 1943 the Muslim League had issued an appeal to the *pirs* of Muslim India to pray and exhort 'their followers to sacrifice their all in the cause of the attainment of a free and independent Muslim India'.[57] It was only after the Simla Conference, however, that large numbers of Sufis responded to this appeal. The *Pirs* of the Chishti revivalist shrines[58] were particularly at the forefront of this movement in the Punjab. They had never been as fully integrated into the Unionist political system as had the *pirs* of the older established shrines.[59] Their *Sajjada Nashins* had been waiting for a long time to put politics in the province on a firmer religious footing. Pir Fazl Shah of Jalalpur had even formed his own party, the *Hizbullah* (Party of God) in the mid-1930s, in order to avoid entanglement with the Unionists. Other *pirs* joined the League at this time for factional political considerations,[60] in response to the communalization of All-India politics and out of a mixture of religious fervour and political self-interest. They provided a traditional channel of communication through which the League could reach illiterate rural voters. The Muslim League was thus able to approach the vital 1946 Provincial Elections in an immeasurably stronger position than it had been nine years earlier.

THE LEAGUE'S VICTORY AT THE POLLS

The 1946 Provincial Elections formed the most crucial period in the Punjab League's history. It had to destroy the Unionist Party's traditional dominance in the rural constituencies in order to prove that the demand for Pakistan was popular in this key area. As in previous elections, in most of the rural constituencies the selection of candidates was more important than the electioneering itself. 'The parties have yet to choose their respective candidates and much thought and study will be needed for this important step in electioneering'. The Editor of the *Civil and Military Gazette* wrote on 4 September 1945, 'The party which chooses a better set of candidates, keeping in view the local alliances and clannish feelings, will, of course, have a tremendous advantage'.[61] Although it had earlier criticized the Unionist Party for using 'tribalism' and the peasants' superstitious reverence for *pirs* to win political support, the Muslim League did not quibble about using these same methods when it was in a position to do so. Like elsewhere in Muslim India it was prepared to pass over local activists in order to field 'men of influence'. Another familiar feature of its campaign was the widespread use of student propagandists.[62] The key to the League's success, however, lay with the landlords and *pirs*. The former used their influence over their tenants, their wealth and their position as tribal chiefs[63] to win votes for the League. The latter appealed to their disciples through '*fatwas*' (religious directives) which were disseminated by means of small leaflets and wall-posters as well as by publication in such Urdu papers as *Nawa-e-Waqt* and *Inqilab*. In them, appeals to vote for the League were often couched solely in terms of the loyalty of a disciple to his *pir* and Sufi order (*silsilah*). The following *fatwa* issued by Syed Fazal Ahmad Shah, *Sajjada Nashin* of the Shrine of Hazrat Shah Nur Jamal, is a good illustration of this:

> An announcement from the *dargah* (*shrine*) of Hazrat Shah Nur Jamal. I command all those people who are in my *silsilah* to do everything possible to help the Muslim League and give their votes to it. All those people who do not act according to this message should consider themselves no longer members of my *silsilah*.
>
> Signed Fazal Ahmad Shah, *Sajjada Nashin* Hazrat Shah Nur Jamal.[64]

Most of the leading shrines issued similar *fatwas* in the Muslim League's support. Significantly, the League received its greatest number of votes in such areas as Jhang, Multan, Jhelum, and Karwal, where it had won over the leading *Pirs*.[65]

The Unionist Party responded to the League's appeal by introducing a religious content into its propaganda. Khizr began to garnish with quotations from the Qur'an his discourses on the economic benefits which the ministry had brought to the countryside. In a speech at Gujrat, for example, he used the first verse of the *Sura Fatiha* to prove that the Unionist Party had a greater Islamic justification than the Muslim League.[66] The Unionist Party flew at its election camps an Islamic flag identical to the League's. Shortly before his death at the end of 1944, Chhotu Ram drew up a plan for employing *ulema* to campaign against the League. Some indeed, worked for the Unionists during the elections. But their influence was weak in the countryside. So with dwindling support amongst the landowners, many of whom adopted a religious garb for the election's duration[67] and with no *pirs* to call upon, the Unionists only feebly imitated the League's Islamic appeals. In the end, they relied heavily on their control of patronage and the machinery of government in a fruitless effort to stem the Muslim League tide.[68]

The election results revealed the Muslim League's rapid advance since 1944. It captured 75 of the 86 Muslim seats, winning all 11 of the urban and 64 of the 75 rural constituencies. The Unionist Party was reduced to a rump of 18 members in the 175-strong Assembly. The League's victory paved the way for Pakistan. It was not able, however, to form a Ministry in the region before Partition, and only unseated the Unionist coalition after a campaign of direct action.

THE PATHWAY TO PARTITION

In Punjab, as in Bengal, there was a conflict after the elections between the needs of ministry-making and local communal peace and the requirements of Jinnah's All-India strategy. The Nawab of Mamdot was as keen to form a coalition ministry in Punjab as was Suhrawardy in Bengal. He not only had to contend with Jinnah's veto, however, but also with the intense animosity towards Pakistan which had been generated by the League's election campaign. In these circumstances the League found it impossible to come to an agreement with Tara Singh, the leader of the Akalis, which was necessary in order to form a viable ministry.[69] In the end Glancy called on Khizr to form a Unionist coalition with the Congress and the Sikhs. The new ministry superficially appeared to have restored the traditional pattern of intercommunal co-operation. In fact it stood in the way of any lasting settlement. The Punjab League leaders were furious at having defeat snatched from the jaws of victory. They hardened their attitude to the minority communities and scarcely concealed their enmity towards the British. The likelihood increased that there would be future violent confrontation within the region.

The Punjab escaped the riots which broke out elsewhere in India after the collapse of the *Cabinet Mission Plan*. At a Governor's Conference held in the wake of the disorders in August 1946, the new Governor Jenkins assured the Viceroy that all the villages which he had recently toured remained 'as friendly as ever' and the rural population appeared unconcerned with politics.[70] But this was the lull before the storm which broke following Attlee's announcement of 20 February 1947. This set a deadline for the transfer of power of June 1948. If constitution-making was not taking place in a 'fully representative Assembly' by that date, His Majesty's Government would hand over power 'in some areas to the existing Provincial Governments'.[71] This raised the possibility of Pakistan being strangled at birth, if a Unionist Coalition ministry was still in power in Punjab. Under the pretext of Khizr's ban on public meetings and on the Muslim League National Guards, the Muslim League stepped up its direct action agitation against the Punjab ministry. Although many leaders were arrested, the campaign built up a popular momentum which made the province almost ungovernable. Like the direct action campaign in the Frontier, it also heightened an already tense communal atmosphere. Whilst direct action ensured that the Muslims would not be denied Pakistan, it also made it inevitable that the Hindus and Sikhs would demand the Partition of the non-Muslim majority districts of East Punjab as its price.

Khizr resigned on 2 March 1947. The prospect of the formation of a Muslim League Government led to serious Sikh demonstrations in Lahore two days later. Rioting spread to the neighbouring Sikh religious centre of Amritsar where 4,000 Muslim shops and businesses were burnt down in the old walled city. The scattered Sikh population of the north-west Punjab bore the brunt of the Muslim desire for revenge. Whole villages were put to the sword. Muslim raids on larger centres of Hindu and Sikh population such as Murree were well organized and in some cases led by retired army officers.[72] The low morale of the predominantly Muslim police force and the unreliability of some officers and men in the Indian 7th Division which had been sent to the disturbed region hampered British efforts to halt the attacks. They claimed nearly 3,000 non-Muslim victims. Another 40,000 Hindus and Sikhs had to shelter in refugee camps which the British set up as soon as they had restored order.

The March riots left a legacy of hatred and distrust. Barricades went up in some of the Punjabi towns. Muslim villagers began to stockpile weapons smuggled in from the Frontier, whilst the Sikhs acquired weapons from the neighbouring Princely States. They harboured a burning desire for revenge. In the countryside they formed armed bands known as *jathas*. These attacked Central Punjab Muslim villages and were to later mercilessly harry Muslim refugees fleeing from Delhi and the East Punjab to Pakistan.

Throughout the spring of 1947, arson and stray assaults were daily occurrences in Amritsar and Lahore. The British had insufficient men to prevent the drift to chaos. The Punjab Security Council which they set up consisting of Muslim, Hindu, and Sikh leaders, issued appeals for communal calm to no avail. Many of the attacks were spontaneous, others were organized by local Muslim and Hindu paramilitary leaders who were out of the control of their provincial political parties. The Nawab of Mamdot finally resigned from the Security Council on 3 July in protest at a heavy-handed British search for weapons in the northern Muslim Misri Shah suburb of Lahore. Trust and goodwill were, in fact, conspicuously lacking at all levels of Punjabi political life as British rule drew to its close. Typical of the animosity were the proceedings of the Provincial Partition Committee which was set up in Lahore under Sir Evan Jenkins' chairmanship. Its task was to ensure a smooth transfer of power by determining the division of assets, personnel, and liabilities before Partition. In the Punjab Governor's words, it set about this task 'very slowly indeed', the Committee's meetings resembling a 'peace conference with a new war in sight'.[73] The war broke out with terrible ferocity, once the last vestiges of British power were removed. Pakistan inherited a Punjab shorn of its fertile eastern districts of Ambala, Jullundur, and Ludhiana, and scarred by massacre and mass migration.

The Muslim League was in a weak position to heal the Punjab's wounds. Even before Independence, the personal rivalries between Firoz Khan Noon, Mian Mumtaz Daultana, and the Nawab of Mamdot were rising to the surface. They were soon to lead to a split which saw the Nawab of Mamdot join with such other 'political outs' as *Pir* Manki and Suhrawardy to form an All-Pakistan Jinnah Awami League. The Punjab League was packed with opportunists in 1947 who had little commitment to the Pakistan ideal. The heart of Unionism's strength, the control of the voters by rural notables and the latter's desire to be left alone to run their local bailiwicks, remained untouched in 1947. Indeed, the Unionist Party's defeat, but not that of Unionism itself, had resulted at least in part from Government's increased intervention in wartime Punjab. Its other major cause had been the fact that in the circumstances of 1945-7, it was no longer seen as the best security for the large landowners' local interests. They had deserted it in great numbers,[74] preferring the protection afforded by the Muslim League. This was yet another demonstration of the Punjabi landlords' remarkable capacity for political accommodation, the history of which can be traced back at least as far as the days of Ranjit Singh.[75] Such expediency was not a firm basis on which to build the Muslim League's control of the region. But outside of the Rawalpindi District where some organizational work had been done, it was all that the League had to start with in the new West Punjab State of Pakistan. As elsewhere in Muslim India, no steps had been taken to institutionalize the support and popular enthusiasm displayed for the Pakistan Movement in 1945-7.

REFERENCE

1. Mian Fazl-i-Husain (1877-1936), lawyer, involved in the early activities of both Punjab Congress and Muslim League. Member Punjab Legislative Council for Muslim landholders' seat. Minister for Education 1921. Revenue Minister 1926. 1930-5 Member of Viceroy's Executive Council.

2. Chhotu Ram (1882-1945). Haryana Jat Lawyer. Active in Jat social and educational institutions. Agriculture Minister 1924. Leader Unionist Party 1930-5. Proponent of agrarian reform and measures to curb the money-lenders' influence.
3. Throughout this part of the province, 'The cardinal principle of the strong owner was that the tenant is a serf, without rights or privileges'. *Attock District Gazetteer*, Lahore, 1909, p. 229.
4. These had been donated by successive governments in order to associate the *pirs* with their rule.
5. Nun, M.M.H., 'Assessment Report of the Pakpattan Tehsil of the Montgomery District', Lahore, 1921, 18 Punjab Proceedings P11372, April 1922, Part A, IOR.
6. Nine Canal Colony Districts had been formed after the massive irrigation programme of the late nineteenth century. This had transformed over six million acres of wasteland in West Punjab into the richest farming area in the whole of the subcontinent.
7. The Ghadr Movement had been founded in the United States by Har Dayal with the aim of overthrowing British rule. Some Ghadrites returned to the Punjab on the outbreak of war, hoping to spark off a mass uprising. They made little headway, however, mainly because of the invaluable support which the Sikh landowners and *Zaildars* gave the British authorities in their policing of the Movement.
8. *Punjab Disorders Inquiry Committee*, Vol. 2, New Delhi, 1976, pp. 157, 169, 173.
9. Born 1869. Lawyer. General Secretary Punjab Provincial Muslim League, November 1907. Opposition to the *Lucknow Pact's* weightage proposals led him to form rival Shafi League in 1916. President Chief Court Bar 1919.
10. Jinnah at the time of the 1927 Unity Conference seemed prepared to trade separate electorates which greatly benefited the Unionists for reservation of seats for Muslims in the Central Legislature.
11. He left Punjab saying, 'I shall never come to the Punjab again; it is such a hopeless place'. Husain, Azim, *Mian Fazl-i-Husain, A Political Biography*, London, 1966, p. 311.
12. The importance which the Unionists attached to the *pirs'* support in 1937 comes out clearly in the words of Mohammad Bashir, the Unionist Party organizer of the Gurdaspur district: 'Villagers, you know, follow these 'Pirs' blindly ... Take care of the 'pirs'. Ask them only to be silent on the matter of the elections ... we don't require their help but that they should not oppose us'. In fact, a number of *pirs* played a leading role as candidates and propagandists for the Unionist Party. The *Pirs* of Shergarh and Shah Jiwana mobilized support for the Unionists in the Canal Colony districts. The rival Gilani and Qureshi *pir* families of Multan carved up the Multan and Shujabad constituencies between them. Fourteen of the leading *Pirs* of the Punjab and its surrounding areas issued an election appeal on the Unionist Party's behalf.
13. Afzal, M.R., *Malik Barkat Ali: His Life and His Writings*, Lahore, 1969, p. 36.
14. He had returned from his post of Deputy Governor of the Reserve Bank of India in 1935. He became Unionist Party leader after Mian Fazl-i-Husain's death in October 1936. He was a leading landowner from the north-west of the Province.
15. *Civil and Military Gazette*, 4 May 1937.
16. *Civil and Military Gazette*, 15 July 1937.
17. *Tribune*, 7 October 1937.
18. The *Punjab Alienation of Land Act (Second Amendment)* and the *Registration of Moneylenders Act* both reduced the moneylenders' influence in 1937. The former measure closed the loophole in the *1901 Act* created by the *benami* transaction. The latter enforced a licensing system for moneylenders. Another reform, the *1938 Restitution of Mortgaged Lands Act*, enabled persons to recover all the land which they had mortgaged before 1901. It was estimated that this would result in over 700,000 acres being

returned to its original owners. Early in September 1938, more than 150,000 cultivators attended the Zamindara Conference which Chhotu Ram held at Lyallpur to demonstrate the support for these reforms.

19. Ispahani, M.A.H., *Quaid-e-Azam Jinnah As I Knew Him,* Karachi, 1966, p. 54 and ff.
20. Zaheer, S., *Light on the League-Unionist Conflict,* Bombay, 1944, p. 19 and ff.
21. *Tribune,* 19 and 23 October 1937.
22. Khaliquzzaman, C., *Pathway to Pakistan,* Lahore, 1961, p. 290.
23. A.Y.K. Daultana to Jinnah, 15 November 1937, QIAP File 255/6 and 255/7 NAP.
24. See extract from the Report of the Sub-Committee appointed to consider applications for affiliation from various provinces and letter of Ghulam Rasul to Secretary All-India Muslim League 15 April 1936. Punjab Provincial Muslim League 1936-9, Vol. 131, Part 4, pp. 20 and 23, FMA.
25. Press message from M.A. Jinnah, p. 32, ibid.
26. Muslim League Council Meetings 1940, Vol. 264, Part 1, p. 52, FMA.
27. Malik Barkat Ali to Jinnah, 4 December 1940, QIAP File 215/60 NAP.
28. Without his support Jinnah would have been unable to secure the amendment to the Civil Disobedience Resolution before the Session, which left the decision to launch such a campaign to the League President.
29. These were Ambala, Hoshiarpur, Shahpur, Jhelum, Mianwali, Jhang, Kangra, Dera Ghazi Khan, Rohtak, and Gujranwala.
30. Mahmud of Ghaznavi's sacking of Somnath Temple was a famous episode in Indian Muslim history. It became a by-word amongst Muslims for unyielding resistance to idolatry, to the Hindus it symbolized Muslim intolerance and ferocity.
31. Punjab Muslim Students Federation, Vol. 230, p. 16, FMA.
32. Report of Mohammad Sadiq: Sheikhupura Student Deputation, 22 July 1941, QIAP File 1099/64 NAP.
33. Conference of the Presidents and Secretaries of the Provincial Muslim Leagues, p. 770 ff., Vol. 326, FMA.
34. Mian Bashir Ahmad to Jinnah, 30 January 1943, QIAP File 1701/29 NAP.
35. Khan Rabb Nawaz Khan to Jinnah, 25 March 1943, QIAP File 379/41 NAP.
36. He died suddenly on 26 October 1942.
37. Mir Maqbool Mahmood, Nawab Muzaffar Khan, and Sikander's son Shaukat all had designs on the Premiership.
38. The most notable defectors were Shaukat Hayat, Mian Mumtaz Daultana, Mian Abdul Aziz, and Sheikh Sadiq Hassan.
39. Until 1944 high prices for wheat and other agricultural produce had compensated the farmers for inflation and shortages of consumer goods. But that autumn a substantial and sustained fall of agricultural prices set in.
40. *Eastern Times,* 28 August 1945.
41. Early in November 1943 the Punjab Assembly unanimously adopted an unofficial resolution to the effect that any attempt to control the price of wheat 'would result' in very keen resentment and discontent among the agriculturalist classes. The Muslim League, free from the constraints of office, could take advantage of wartime discontent in a similar way to which the Frontier Congress undermined Aurangzeb Khan's League Ministry.
42. Chhotu Ram was an outspoken critic of the requisitioning of grains, and the placing of a price ceiling on them. Glancy, the Governor, backed up his Ministers, but Wavell wrote back 'To put it quite clearly, the procurement of the necessary surplus wheat from the Punjab is more important than any interests of the Ministers'. The pressures of the Bengal famine thus signalled the end of the traditional policy of putting the Punjab's rural stability above all other considerations.
43. The Sikh community's increased wartime influence was symbolized by Sikander's agreement with Baldev Singh in June 1942 and the latter's entry into the Cabinet.

44. *Eastern Times,* 28 October 1945.
45. Report of the Punjab Provincial Muslim League's work for June and July 1948 submitted to the All-India Muslim League Committee of Action, 28 July 1944, SHC Punjab Vol. 1.
46. Punjab FR, 23 August 1944, L/P&J/5/247 IOR.
47. *Eastern Times,* 23 May 1943.
48. *Nawa-e-Waqt,* 30 April 1943.
49. Mian Mumtaz Daultana to Jinnah, 15 June 1945. SHC Punjab Vol. 3.
50. This was summed up in the following *Editorial:* 'The extent to which the Muslim League will be able to exploit the influence of families and clans in the service of its main election slogan in the individual constituencies will determine not only the future course of politics in this province, but also to a large extent the future of India'. *Eastern Times,* 6 September 1945.
51. Growing support for the Pakistan Movement amongst the tenants and labourers of some landowners led a few of them to decide in this instance to follow the wishes of their clients. The League held some particularly success-ful rural meetings in the Sheikhupura and Montgomery districts in July 1944.
52. Wavell to Amery, 18 April 1944, Mansergh, N. (editor), *The Transfer of Power 1942-7,* Vol. 4, London, 1973, p. 898.
53. Glancy to Wavell, 16 April 1944, Mansergh, op. cit., 1973, p. 881.
54. The August offer declared that the British would not contemplate the transfer of power to any government 'whose authority is directly denied by large and powerful elements in India's national life'. The *Cripps Mission* proposals included an option clause for provincial non-accession to any new constitutional position. Hodson, H.V., *The Great Divide, Britain, India, Pakistan,* London, 1969, p. 85.
55. Report of the Organizing Secretary Rawalpindi Division Muslim League. Punjab Muslim League 1943-4, Vol. 162, Part 7, p. 74 and ff., FMA.
56. Punjab FR for the second half of July 1945, L/P&J/5/247 IOR.
57. G.F. Ansari to Jinnah, 25 April 1943, *QIAP* File 1101/105 R, NAP.
58. The main revivalists' shrines were at Taunsa, Golra, Sial, and Jalalpur. They had been founded during the late eighteenth century by a reform movement which aimed to bring Sufis and *ulema* together and make the shrines centres of Islamic piety as well as popular devotionalism.
59. *Pirs* from older established shrines held offices as *Zaildars,* honorary magis-trates, and were members of the Provincial *Darbar,* like for example the *Diwan* of Pakpattan.
60. The Gilanis of Multan joined the League as part of their traditional rivalry with the pro-Unionist Qureshis.
61. *Civil and Military Gazette,* 4 September 1945.
62. During the peak of student activity, the 1945 Christmas vacation, there were 1,550 members of the Punjab Muslim Students' Federation and 250 Aligarh Students working on the League's behalf.
63. The Arain landowner, Mian Nurullah, for example, used his influence amongst his Arain kinsmen who formed a large part of the electorate in the Lyallpur constituency in order to secure a League victory.
64. *Nawa-e-Waqt,* 19 January 1946.
65. Khalid Saifullah, the editor of the pro-League *Eastern Times,* declared almost immediately after the elections: 'What are the factors that have brought about the revolution in the Pakistani lands? What has made the great change possible? In my view the greatest praise must be lavished, as far as the Punjab is concerned, on the Pirs ... who when they saw the Pakistani nation in mortal danger, emerged from their cells and enjoined upon their followers to resist evil and vote for the League and Pakistan'. *Eastern Times,* 15 March 1946.
66. Khizr's point was that Allah is described in the Qur'an as *Rabb-al-Alumeen,* Lord of everything and everyone, not just the Muslims. In this light, the Unionist Party's non-communalism was more Islamic than the League's communalism.

67. The Nawab of Mamdot, for example, became *Pir* Mamdot Sharif; Shaukat Hayat, the *Sajjada Nashin* of Darbar Sargodha Sharif.
68. In both the Toba Tek Singh and Lyallpur constituencies, individual voters were contacted by the police and government officials and persuaded to support the Unionist Party. In the neighbouring Samundri seat, the Police Superintendent, Waryam Singh, was particularly open in his support for the Unionists. Influential Muslim Leaguers were entangled in legal cases in the hope that this would intimidate voters. The Samundri *Tehsildar* called a meeting of all *lambardars* and *zaildars* on 3 January and warned that they would be dismissed and have their supplies of canal water withheld if they opposed the Unionists. Abdul Bari to Jinnah, 23 January 1946, SHC Punjab 1.
69. The Akalis had won 21 seats, Unionists 21 (3 subsequently defected), Congress 51, and Muslim League 75. There were also 7 Independents in the 175-strong Assembly.
70. Moon, P. (editor), *Wavell: The Viceroy's Journal,* London, 1973, p. 37 and ff.
71. Khizr realized that the announcement would spark off a scramble for power injurious to communal peace and called the statement 'the work of lunatics'.
72. Jenkins to Wavell, 17 March 1947, R/3/1/176 IOR.
73. Note by Jenkins, 11 July 1947, R/3/1/176 IOR.
74. There had also been dramatic conversions from the Punjab Congress during this period. The wealthy President of the Punjab Congress, Mian Iftikhar-ud-din, defected, as did a former President, Malik Lal Khan. When the Khateeb of the mosque of the Sadar *bazaar* in Lahore announced his resignation from the Congress, he was led in a triumphant procession through the *bazaar,* garlanded in currency notes. See *Eastern Times,* 11 January 1046.
75. Firoz Khan Noon's defection to the Muslim League in 1945 followed a long family tradition of political opportunism. The Noon family's tribal head served in Ranjit Singh's army and held several villages in *jagir* as a result. He, however, deserted the Sikh cause in favour of the British during the Sikh wars.

Conclusion

Considerable controversy[1] surrounds the role of Islam in Indian Muslim politics of the 1930s and 1940s. Writers such as Paul Brass[2] maintain that Islam's role was instrumental, that is Islamic ideology was chosen and manipulated by political elites in order to legitimize their bid for power which arose from other, predominantly social and economic, compulsions. Ayesha Jalal[3] has seen Islam as having an illusory explanatory power for understanding the conduct of Muslim politics. Local political traditions of feud and faction rather than the ideology of the Pakistan demand drove forward the Muslim League Movement. Hafeez Malik,[4] I.H. Qureishi[5] and more recently Riazul Islam[6] have in direct contrast seen Islam as the major explanatory factor behind the creation of Pakistan. Their view that Islam does not only legitimize, but also impels, political action and behaviour has been strengthened by the emergence of Islamic fundamentalism in large areas of the Muslim world. This study has shown that Islam's role in the Pakistan Movement was neither wholly instrumental nor illusory, nor was it, however, the sole impelling factor. The voters of Muslim India supported the League in the crucial 1946 elections, not only because of its Islamic appeal. If religion alone had determined the outcome, the Punjab Unionist Party and National Muslim Parliamentary Party of Bengal would have done much better. They both introduced Islamic appeals into their propaganda and had the backing of both *pirs* and *ulema*. The key to the League's success lay rather in its linking of Islamic appeals with solutions to the rural population's economic and social difficulties and its utilization of the traditional rural idiom and channels of communication to put its message across. The *biraderi* networks and Sufi networks together played a vital part in the League's ability to turn the tables on its rivals. Whilst Jinnah naturally depicted the election results as a straightforward verdict on Pakistan, they had as much to do with the League's skilful selection of candidates who possessed 'influence' in the countryside.[7]

On the other hand, however, it would be foolish to deny the importance of a growing sense of Muslim community and brotherhood (asbiyyat) during the final stages of the Pakistan Movement. Revulsion at the Hindu attacks on the Muslim minorities in Bombay and Bihar played an important part in undermining support for G.M. Sayed and his followers in Sind and for the Khan brothers in the Frontier. Muslim elites were not so fancy-free in their choice of community symbols as Paul Brass would have us believe, or as wholly opportunistic and cynical as Ayesha Jalal maintains. The changing national political context of 1945-6 presented the regional Muslim elites with choices of a religious as well as a political nature. Should they be under Muslim or Hindu government? How best was the integrity of the Muslim community to be maintained? Where did their primary allegiance lie—to their faith or to their ethnic and linguistic grouping? Undoubtedly large numbers of Muslims in both Punjab and Bengal had not in 1946 fully grasped the implications of Pakistan for their region. But they were not merely manipulating religion for their own purposes. There was widespread and sincere support for the Pakistan demand which went well beyond the privileged 'elite' of Muslim voters in 1946.[8] Pakistan's political problems since Independence have stemmed not from the Muslim League's cynical manipulation of religion in 1946, but from its failure to establish an effective organization which could give permanence to the enthusiasm for a separate Muslim state.

The Muslim League was poorly organized throughout most of the 'Pakistan areas' on the eve of Independence. Even in Bengal where it had built on the groundwork prepared by

Praja Party activists, local branches were only effectively functioning in 18 out of 27 districts in 1945. Elsewhere, the situation was much worse. The Sind League had just 48,500 members after the purge of G.M. Sayed's followers early in 1946. In the Punjab, the 'cornerstone' of Pakistan, League membership stood at just 150,000, whilst in the neighbouring North-West Frontier Province even its own inspectors had to admit that 'there was no organization worth the name'. Moreover, the tendency of local officials to bolster their influence, by enrolling bogus members, may mean that even these modest totals overestimate the League's true membership. Its provincial branches were further handicapped by lack of funds, paid workers, and sound techniques of office management.

The League's low membership was partly the result of the poor communications and social backwardness of the rural regions of the Pakistan areas. Another important factor, however, was the desire for quick results after the debacle of 1937. League officials rather than embarking on the slow and painful process of building up grassroots support, turned to the rural notables with their readymade networks of clients. The policy succeeded in the short term as the League was able to secure morale raising victories in bye-elections and to form ministries in Sind and the Frontier. In the long term, however, it had serious drawbacks. Future mass contact work in the countryside was made difficult. Landed League officials such as the Nawab of Dacca or the Nawab of Mamdot, were just as obstructive to organizational work as were the Unionist landowners of the Punjab. They branded as Communists officials like Abul Hashim who attempted to raise the political consciousness of the villagers. Whilst they were willing to lend their influence to the League in All-India affairs, they tried to keep it at arm's length in their home districts. The resulting slow growth of organization in the districts made it difficult for the League to curb the factionalism and nepotism of the landowners, or to bring them in line with its official policy. Those Leaguers whose concept of Pakistan bore closest resemblance to Jinnah's own, men such as Malik Barkat Ali and Ispahani, were frequently excluded from the Provincial Leagues' Inner Councils, as they did not possess a rural powerbase.

Factionalism and corruption, although not the monopoly of landowners, increased with their entry into the Muslim League's ranks. The Khans brought with them the Frontier code of *taburwali*. In Bengal, the Nawab of Dacca's brother Shahabuddin discredited the League with his notorious corruption.[9] Mir Bandeh Ali's Mir Ministers in Sind brought 'undue pressure' on revenue and police officials 'to achieve their personal gains'. They obtained votes by ensuring that confiscated gun licences were returned to *'badmash zamindars'* and 'let the public go to hell' in their anxiety to increase their property.[10] Factional struggles between 'ins' and 'outs' frequently widened into a tussle between ministers and Party officials. The Frontier League was paralysed by such a contest and whilst a compromise was achieved in Bengal, in Sind a split occurred on the eve of the 1946 Provincial Elections.

Jinnah remained aloof from these struggles, not because he was the impotent bystander which Ayesha Jalal maintains,[11] but because he did not want to tarnish the All-India Muslim League's reputation by becoming too closely involved with the day-to-day squabbles of the provincial politicians. Even immediately after the abysmal showing of the 1937 elections, Jinnah was not totally at the mercy of the regional leaders. Sikander's support of the October Lucknow Session was a timely boost which carried with it a high price. But Fazlul Huq was as much in need of Jinnah's support at the provincial level of politics as Jinnah required his at the Centre. As the League's prestige rose during the Second World War, Jinnah's authority increased in his dealings with the majority area leaders. Sikander and Huq both complied with his request and resigned from the Viceroy's Executive Council in July 1941. Hidayatullah dropped Moula Baksh when asked to do so in March 1945. On two occasions in 1946, Suhrawardy did not go ahead with plans to form a coalition with the Congress, because it met with Jinnah's disapproval.

Indeed, from the time of the Simla Conference onwards regional parties and interests took second place to the All-India Muslim League. The Punjab Unionist Party was the greatest victim of the League's post-Simla authority. Its support in the Assembly dramatically crumbled. In Bengal and the Frontier also there were sizeable defections to the Muslim League. The fierce struggle for League election tickets in Bengal and Sind was further evidence of the traditional elite's realization that there would be no access to power outside its ranks.

Although popular enthusiasm for Pakistan remained unorganized, the late entry of large numbers of landowners into the League's ranks enabled it to control the traditional channels of political mobilization. The League thus swept to victory in the key areas of Punjab and Bengal in the 1946 Provincial Elections. Jinnah was dealt a strong hand in his negotiations for Pakistan. The Muslim League's real position in the majority areas, however, was much weaker than it appeared. This was to have damaging long-term consequences.

The provincial Muslim Leagues instead of laying their foundations on the rock of sound organization had built them on the shifting sands of elite factionalism. The rural elite's traditional rivalries and particularisms had only been temporarily submerged at a crisis point in the All-India Muslim League's struggle with the Congress and the British. Opportunist converts could jump off the League bandwagon as quickly as they had scrambled on board it. Jinnah's untimely death compounded the problems brought by mounting factionalism within Punjab and the revival of traditional opponents in the Frontier and Sind. By 1956 the League was in rapid decline. Whilst its organizational weakness had not prevented the birth of Pakistan, it was to severely jeopardize the task of nation-building.

REFERENCE

1. For a discussion of this see Shaikh, F., 'Muslims and Political Representation in Colonial India—The Making of Pakistan', in *Modern Asian Studies,* 20, 3, July 1986.
2. Brass, Paul, *Language, Religion and Politics in North India,* Cambridge, 1974.
3. Jalal, op. cit., 1985, see for example p. 151.
4. Malik, H., *Moslem Nationalism in India and Pakistan,* Washington, 1963.
5. Qureishi, I.H., *The Struggle for Pakistan,* Karachi, 1965.
6. Islam, R., 'The Religious Factor in the Pakistan Movement', *Proceedings on the First Congress on the History and Culture of Pakistan,* Vol. 3, Islamabad, 1976.
7. The League's Central Parliamentary Board took a realistic attitude almost bordering on outright cynicism in its recommendation for tickets in 1945-6.
8. A study of the Pakistan Movement at the mass rather than the elite level is urgently called for, with an emphasis on popular demonstrations, processions, and strikes rather than legislative politics and party organization, and with an emphasis on the 'subaltern classes', industrial labourers, *haris,* and women, rather than landowners.
9. Raghib Ahsan to Jinnah, 11 July 1944, *QIAP* F1102.
10. Ghulam Kadirshah to Jinnah, 4 March 1941, *QIAP* F1261.
11. Jalal, op. cit., 1985, see for example pp. 111, 114, 116.

Appendices

Appendices

APPENDIX A

The Muslim League in Baluchistan

Baluchistan was the most backward region of Muslim India. As late as 1944 it had only four Government High Schools and a literacy rate of under 2 per cent.[1] Its Muslim population was overwhelmingly rural. Quetta, the largest town, had under 35,000 inhabitants, half of which were non-Muslim. The province was unable to sustain itself and relied heavily on Central Government loans of around 60 lakh rupees by the early 1940s. Political backwardness went hand-in-hand with its low level of economic and social development. Electoral politics were restricted to Quetta Municipality right down to Independence. Baluchistan's decision to join Pakistan was decided by just 54 members of the *Shahi Jirga* and five members of the Quetta Municipality (The Council of Tribal Leaders). Despite this backwardness, the Muslim League attached considerable importance to the region. Baluchistan was included in all Pakistan Schemes from Iqbal's December 1930 All-India Muslim League Presidential Address onwards. Jinnah included democratic reforms for Baluchistan in his famous 'fourteen points' of 1928. He visited Quetta on two occasions during the final stages of the Pakistan campaign, in June 1943 and October 1945.

The son of the *Sardar* of the Magsi Tribe, Yusuf Ali Khan Magsi, began the first stirrings of political organization in Baluchistan during the early 1930s. Significantly, the centre of his attention was not a national issue, but over who should succeed as the ruler of Kalat State. Yusuf founded a number of newspapers which were devoted to Baluchi affairs, although they were published in Karachi and Lahore. He joined a political organization, the *Anjuman-i-Ittehad-i-Baluchen*,[2] became its President and organized the First All-India Baluch Conference at Jacobabad in December 1932. Yusuf's growing political influence was tragically cut short, by his death in the 1935 Quetta earthquake.

The *Anjuman-i-Ittehad-i-Baluchen* and its successor, the Kalat State National Party, collaborated during the late 1930s with Baluchistan's other political organization, the *Anjuman-i-Watan*. This was founded by a Pathan, Abdus Samad Achakzai, who also ran the *Istiqlal* newspaper. The *Anjuman-i-Watan* virtually functioned as the Baluchistan branch of the Congress. The Muslim League, as in the other majority areas, was a latecomer. Its creation in June 1939 was the result of the single-handed efforts of a Quetta lawyer, Qazi Mohammad Isa.

Qazi Mohammad Isa established the Baluchistan Muslim League at a meeting in a mosque held in Pishin.[3] He wanted to dispose with the creation of a Working Committee and other office holders 'because once these office holders are announced, I would at once create an opposition, which would not be an opposition to the cause, but the personage so appointed'. The fact that the League was a one-man band would not reduce the spread of its influence, for 'when a district or village I want to tour, I [shall] pick up persons who are very influential there and through them make these people understand'.[4] The All-India Muslim League Council at Delhi, however, would not permit the affiliation of the Baluchistan League, until it had properly constituted itself. Isa duly produced a 25-page constitution with provision for a popularly elected League organization down to the village level.[5] This remained, however, a paper organization.

Isa was rewarded for his efforts by becoming a member of the new All-India Muslim League Working Committee, set up after the passing of the *Lahore Resolution*. He was later to serve as a member of the Committee of Action, and Central Parliamentary Board. The First Annual Session of the Baluchistan Provincial Muslim League was held in July 1940 under the Presidentship of Nawabzada Liaquat Ali Khan. It reiterated the demand for the introduction of political reforms within the province. Two years elapsed, before a second session was held under the presidentship of the Nawab of Mamdot. During this time propaganda was confined to the columns of Isa's *Al-Islam* newspaper, as the League became virtually moribund. No subscriptions were collected from members from 1940 onwards, and no new members were enrolled; local branches were non-existent.[6] Jinnah's visit to Baluchistan in June 1943, however, temporarily galvanized the League back into life. The Quaid was borne through Quetta city like a 'royal potentate' in a large procession estimated to number 50,000 persons. The entire route was decorated with welcome arches and gateways named after Muslim heroes. On 3 July, Jinnah addressed the Annual Session of the Baluchistan League which was attended by a large number of tribal *Sardars* and Nawabs. He then went on to stay as the guest of the ruler of Kalat, Mir Ahmed Yar Khan. One by-product of Jinnah's visit was the establishment of the Baluchistan Muslim Students Federation in October.

After the excitements of 1943, the League settled down to its usual torpor when Khair Mohammad of the Students Federation attempted to stir it to life. He 'created a bad impression' and new student office bearers and a touring party were selected by the gentry of Quetta at a tea-party held by Mohammad Azam Khan Kasi.[7] A further row was caused early in 1944, over Isa's 'domination' of the Baluchistan League. By this date he was out of the Province for much of the time on All-India Muslim League business. While he was absent, a number of tribal leaders began to question his right to represent Baluchistan when he was neither a Baluchi nor a *Sardar*. They also objected to the fact that almost the entire Provincial League Council came from Quetta and was Mohammad Qazi Isa's nominees.[8] Although Liaquat Ali Khan backed Isa's side of the argument in 1944, the discontent lingered and Isa was forced to waive his claim to be Baluchistan's representative in the proposed B Grouping of Provinces of the *Cabinet Mission Plan*.

The Muslim League stepped up its activities in Baluchistan, as elsewhere in India, following the collapse of the Simla Conference. The Quetta city Muslim League held a conference in late September 1945 which was addressed by the Punjabi leader Firoz Khan Noon. Although it only attracted 3,000 persons,[9] this was much larger than the attendances at *Anjuman-i-Watan* public meetings.[10] In October, Jinnah made another successful visit to the province. He once again called for further political reform and highlighted the League's championing of this cause. Although there was no election campaign to be fought in Baluchistan in 1946, the League kept up its efforts to counteract the Congress and persuade the *Sardars* that their future lay with Pakistan. Early in 1947 the League held meetings at Quetta, Fort Sandeman and Nushki, where a new branch organization was formed.[11] An 'almost complete' *hartal* (strike) was held in Quetta on 29 January to protest about the arrest of Muslim League leaders during the direct action campaign in Lahore. Regular drilling of Muslim League National Guards took place in Quetta.

All this was a dress rehearsal for the popular pressure the League exerted on the members of the *Shahi Jirga* which met, along with the Quetta Municipality, on 30 June 1947, to decide whether Baluchistan should join Pakistan. The Congress had played on the fear that Pakistan would be too poor to support the deficit province, its delegation had also attempted to set Baluchis off against Pathans, whilst holding out the hope of eventual independence. The League counteracted this 'bitter' propaganda by taking out a huge procession in Quetta on 23 June.[12] To further impress the tribal elders of the *Shahi Jirga* who were in the city, the League persuaded Nawab Jogezai, the scion of a former ruling family of Baluchistan, to place himself at its head. On the day on which the vote was to take place, the League gathered a huge crowd outside the Town Hall. Inside it all the 54 members present voted[13] to join the Pakistan Constituent Assembly 'mindful of the emotions and feelings of the people of Baluchistan'.

REFERENCE

1. The Province of Baluchistan covered on area of 134, 638 square miles. Its population in 1944 was 868,617; 91 per cent of which was Muslim. It spoke six main languages, Baluchi, Pushtu, Sindhi, Bruhi, Lahnda, and Persian. Its six districts were under the control of an Agent. Surrounding the province were the Tribal Areas of Marri and Bugti and the states of Kalat, Kharan, Makran, and Lasbela.
2. This was founded in 1930 by Abdul Aziz Kurd, an editor of one of Yusuf's newspapers.
3. Qazi Mohammad Isa to Liaquat Ali Khan, 16 June 1939, Baluchistan Muslim League, 1939-44, Vol. 293, FMA.
4. Ibid.

120   APPENDIX A

5. Each village was to have an elected President and Secretary, and a Village Council of six to ten members.
6. Mir Jaffar Khan Jamali to Jinnah, 31 March 1944. Qazi Mohammad Isa to Liaquat Ali Khan, 16 June 1939. Baluchistan Muslim League, 1939-44, Vol. 293, FMA.
7. K.S. Mohammad Azam Khan Kasi to Qazi Mohammad Isa, December 1945, Baluchistan Provincial Muslim League 1946-7, Part III, Vol. 371, FMA.
8. Mir Jaffar Khan Jamali to Jinnah, 31 March 1944.
9. *Baluchistan Agent's Report*, first half of October 1945, L/P&J/5/276 IOR.
10. A public meeting held in Quetta in June 1945 was attended by just 125 people. *Baluchistan Agent's Report*, second half of June 1945, L/P&J/5/276.
11. *Baluchistan Agent's Report*, second half of March 1947, L/P&J/5/278 IOR.
12. I.H. Kausar, *Pakistan Movement in Baluchistan*, Karachi, n.d., p. 44 and ff.
13. Three members of the *Shahi Jirga* and five out of the ten members of the Quetta Municipality were absent.

Muslim Population by Province and District

Table 2.1: Muslim Percentage of Total Population by District Bengal 1931

District	Muslims
Burdwan	19.07
Birbhum	28.05
Bankura	4.8
Midnapore	7.8
Hooghly	16.3
Howrah	21.3
24-Parganas	34.4
Calcutta	27.4
Nadia	62.2
Murshidabad	56.4
Jessore	62.0
Khulna	49.6
Rajshahi	76.9
Jalpaiguri	26.2
Darjeeling	3.3
Rangpur	71.1
Bogra	83.6
Pabna	77.6
Malda	56.3
Dacca	67.1
Mymensingh	76.9
Faridpur	64.0
Backerganj	72.0
Tippera	75.4
Noakhali	78.5
Chittagong	77.1
Chittagong Hill Tracts	16.2

Source: Census of India 1931, Vol. V, Bengal and Sikkim, Part 2, p. 160.

Table 2.2: **Muslim Distribution by District—North-West Frontier Province 1931 (Percentage of)**

District	Pathan Total Population	Non-Pathan Muslims	Total Muslims
Hazara	8.14	86.89	95.03
Peshawar	48.62	44.64	93.26
Kohat	62.68	29.77	92.45
Bannu	59.10	28.23	87.33
D.I. Khan	25.18	60.82	86.00
Total	37.32	54.52	91.84

Source: Compiled from *Census of India 1931*, Vol. X, Part 1, pp. 187 and 201.

Table 2.3: **Muslim Distribution by District—Sind 1931**

District	Muslim Total Population (Percentage of)
Karachi	73.9
Hyderabad	69.9
Nawabshah	76.5
Larkana	83.6
Sukkur	71.3
Tharparkar	52.9
Upper Sind Frontier	89.9
Total	73.6

Source: Census of India 1931, Vol. VIII, Part 1, p. 368.

Provincial Assembly Results,
Bengal, Punjab, North-West Frontier Province, 1946

MUSLIM URBAN AND RURAL CONSTITUENCIES

Table 3.1: **Bengal**

Constituency	Name and Party of Successful Candidate	Percentage of the Total Vote
MUHAMMADAN URBAN		
Calcutta North	Mohammad Rafique (ML)	98.4
Calcutta South	K. Nuruddin (ML)	unopposed
Hooghly cum Howrah Municipality	Mohammad Sarif Khan (ML)	93.1
Barrackpore Municipal	Mohammad Qumruddin (ML)	83.2
24-Parganas Municipal	H.S. Suhrawardy (ML)	unopposed
Dacca Municipal	Nawabzada K. Nasarullah (ML)	98.9
Total Muslim League Percentage of Urban Muslim votes cast		95.0
MUHAMMADAN RURAL		
Burdwan	Abdul Hashim (ML)	96.4
Birbhum	K.B. Mudassar Hossain (ML)	unopposed
Bankura	Syed Muhammad Siddique (ML)	79.4
Midnapore	Serajuddin Ahmad (ML)	unopposed
Hooghly	Abdul Quasem (ML)	unopposed
Howrah	Mohammad Idris (ML)	99.9
24-Parganas South	Jasimuddin Ahmad (ML)	72.2
24-Parganas Central	Ilias Ali Molla (ML)	99.1
24-Parganas North East	K.B. Abdur Rahman (ML)	76.3
Kushtia	Shamsuddin Ahmed (ML)	95.4
Meherpore	Abdul Hannan (ML)	97.1
Nadia East	Abdul Mataleb Malik (ML)	98.1
Nadia West	Molla Mohd Abdul Halum (ML)	97.5
Berhampore	Mohd Khuda Bukhsh (Inde)	58.1
Murshidabad South West	Sahibzada K J Saiyid Kazim Ali Mirza (ML)	93.2
Jangipur	Mortaza Raza Choudhury (ML)	94.9
Jessore Sadar	Lutfar Rahman (ML)	95.1
Jessore East	Abdul Awal (ML)	82.1
Bongaun	Serajul Islam (ML)	96.2
Jhenidah	Tafazzel Hossain (ML)	92.9
Khulna	Abdus Sabar Khan (ML)	90.9

continued

Table 3.1 continued

Constituency	Name and Party of Successful Candidate	Percentage of the Total Vote
Satkhira	Abdul Ahad (ML)	88.2
Bagerhat	Fazlul Huq (Krishak Praja)	49.2
Natore	Kaji Abdul Masud (ML)	96.4
Rajshahi North	Maniruddin Akanda (ML)	81.2
Rajshahi South	Abdul Hamid (ML)	93.1
Rajshahi Central	Madar Buk (ML)	53.8
Balurghat	Mazaffar Rahman Choudhury (ML)	92.2
Thakurgaon	Hafizuddin Choudhury (ML)	unopposed
Dinajpur Central-East	Mohammad Abdullaheh Baqui (ML)	74.4
Dinajpur Central-West	Hassan Ali (ML)	84.8
Jalpaiguri *cum* Darjeeling	Nawab Musharraf Hossain (ML)	79.8
Nilphamari	Khairat Hossain (ML)	98.0
Rangpur North	Mohammad Oswais (ML)	98.7
Rangpur South	Emad Uddin Ahammad (ML)	94.6
Kurigaon North	Paniruddin Ahmad (ML)	93.2
Kurigaon South	Nazir Hossain Khandakar (ML)	86.5
Gaibandha North	Serajuddin Ahmed (ML)	70.8
Gaibandha South	Ahammad Hossain (ML)	92.4
Bogra East	Badiazzahan Muhd. Elias (ML)	61.6
Bogra South	Muhammad Ishaque (ML)	97.1
Bogra North	Mobarak Ali Ahamed (ML)	97.1
Bogra West	K.B. Mohammad Ali (ML)	98.6
Pabna East	Dewan Lutfar Ali (ML)	94.9
Pabna West	K.B.A.M. Abdul Hamid (ML)	unopposed
Serajganj South	Abdur Rashid Mahmood (ML)	76.4
Serajganj North	K.S. Osman Gani (ML)	72.3
Serajganj Central	Abdur Rashid Khodker (ML)	93.5
Malda North	Mohd Sayed Mia (ML)	94.1
Malda South	Zahed Ahmed Choudhury (ML)	86.8
Narayanganj South	Osman Ali (ML)	85.6
Narayanganj East	Maulana Mohd Abdul Aziz (ML)	94.2
Narayanganj North	Syed Abdus Salim (ML)	93.7
Munshiganj	Muhd Abdul Hakim Vikrampuri (ML)	99.4
Dacca South Central	K.B. Abdul Khaleque (ML)	97.8
Manikganj East	K.B. Aulad Hossain Khan (ML)	92.8
Manikganj West	Masihuddin Ahmed (ML)	87.3
Dacca North Central	Fakir Abdul Mannan (ML)	89.7

continued

Table 3.1 continued

Constituency	Name and Party of Successful Candidate	Percentage of the Total Vote
Dacca Central	Abu Taiyab Mazharul Haque (ML)	74.3
Jamalpur East	K.B. Fazlur Rahman (ML)	66.0
Jamalpur North	Abdul Karim (ML)	69.7
Jamalpur West	A.K.M. Bafatuddin (ML)	95.8
Jamalpur cum Muktagalha	Ahammad Ali Mir (ML)	89.4
Mymensingh North	K.B. Surafuddin Ahmed (ML)	98.6
Mymensingh East	K.B. Nurul Amin (ML)	88.5
Mymensingh South	Maulana Shamsul Huda (Inde)	67.7
Mymensingh West	Abdul Kalam Shamsuddin (ML)	unopposed
Tangail South	Khurram Khan Panee (ML)	98.0
Tangail West	Abdul Hafizmirza (ML)	90.3
Tangail North	K.B. Ebrahim Khan (ML)	97.4
Netrakona South	Asanali Mukter (ML)	98.0
Netrakona North	Moulvi Akbar Ali (ML)	96.3
Kishoreganj South	Mohd Israil (ML)	57.3
Kishoreganj North	Syed Habibul Haque (ML)	93.5
Kishoreganj East	K.S. Hamiddudin Ahmed (ML)	97.8
Gopalganj	Shamsuddin Ahmed Khandkar (ML)	77.5
Gorlundo	Ahmed Ali Mridha (ML)	80.6
Faridpur West	K.B. Yusuf Hossain Choudhury (ML)	76.8
Faridpur East	Shamsuddin Ahmed (Inde)	51.6
Madaripur West	Eskander Ali Khan (ML)	89.6
Madaripur East	K.S. Abdul Aziz Munshi (ML)	77.5
Patuakhali North	Abdur Rahman Khan (ML)	60.4
Patuakhali South	Mohd Shamsuddin Sidker (ML)	68.9
Pirojpur South	K.S. Hatem Ally (Krishak Praja)	51.2
Pirojpur North	K.B. Syed Mohd-Afzal (Krishak Praja)	73.9
Bakarganj North	Mohd-Ariff Choudhury (ML)	67.2
Bakarganj South	Fazlul Huq (Krishak Praja)	76.9
Bakarganj West	Moulana Haji Mohd-Quasem (ML)	49.4
Bhola North	K.B. Nuruzzaman (ML)	73.6
Bhola South	Syed Azizur Rahman (ML)	83.5
Brahmanbaria North	Muhd. Rakonuddin (ML)	98.9
Brahmanbaria South	Ali Ahmad Khan (ML)	96.1
Tippera North-East	Tafazzal Ali (ML)	96.4
Tippera North	K.S. Mafizuddin Ahmed (ML)	94.2

continued

Table 3.1 continued

Constituency	Name and Party of Successful Candidate	Percentage of the Total Vote
Tippera West	Nowab Ali (ML)	95.1
Tippera Central	Abdul Momin (ML)	86.4
Tippera South	Syed Serajal Haque (ML)	88.4
Chandpur East	Janabali Mia (ML)	95.6
Chandpur West	K.B. Abidur Rezachaudhury (ML)	99.0
Matiabbazar	Muhd Abdus Salam (ML)	95.8
Noakhali North	Fazlur Rahman (ML)	76.8
Noakhali Central	Majibar Rahman (ML)	87.8
Ramganj *cum* Raipur	Fazluh Karim (ML)	82.7
Noakhali West	Abdul Hakim Mia (ML)	88.4
Noakhali South	Abdul Hai (ML)	99.3
Feni	Muhd Habibullah Choudhury (ML)	84.5
Cox's Bazar	Kabir Ahmad Choudhury (ML)	83.8
Chittagong South-East	Shmed Karib Choudhury (ML)	98.2
Chittagong South-Central	Ali Ahmed Choudhury (ML)	91.1
Chittagong North-East	K.B. Farid Ahmed Choudhury (ML)	89.9
Chittagong North-West	Fazlul Qadir (ML)	unopposed

Total Muslim League percentage of Rural Muslim Votes cast 83.8

Source: Compiled from *Return Showing Results of Elections to the Central Legislative Assembly and Provincial Assemblies in 1945-6,* New Delhi, 1948, p. 110 and ff.

Table 3.2: North-West Frontier Province Provincial Assembly Results
        1946

Constituency	Name and Party of Successful Candidate	Percentage of the Total Vote
MUHAMMADAN URBAN		
Peshawar City	Muhammad Yahya Jan (Cong)	28.6
(Dual Constituency)	Abdul Aniyum Khan (ML)	23.1
N.W.F.P. Towns	K.B. Jalaluddin (ML)	55.5
MUHAMMADAN RURAL		
Tanawal	Muhd. Farid Khan of Bir (ML)	32.7
Abbottabad West	Lt. Zain Muhammad Khan (ML)	48.7
Abbottabad East	K.B. Abdur Rahman Khan (ML)	91.4
Haripur North	K.B. Muhammad Zaman Khan (ML)	47.8
Haripur Central	Sardar Bahadur Khan (ML)	41.2
Haripur South	Raja Haidar Zaman Khan (ML)	47.8
Mansehra North	Muhd Abbas Khan (ML)	45.7
Upper Pakhli	Abdul Qaiyum Khan (Cong)	35.1
Lower Pakhli	Ali Gohar Khan (ML)	40.8
Bara Mohmands	Arab Muhd Sharif Khan of Ladi (ML)	52.1
Khalils	Amin Jan Khan (Cong)	51.2
Hashtnagar North	Syed Qaim Shah (Cong)	52.3
Hashtnagar South	Dr. Khan Sahib (Cong)	78.7
Doaba Daudzai South	Arbab Abdur Rahman Khan (Cong)	70.9
Nowshera South	Mian Jafar Shah (Cong)	58.2
Nowshera North	Syed Yakub Shah (Cong)	63.9
Baizai	Muhd Zarin Khan (Cong)	47.1
Kamalzai	Nawab Muhd Akbar Khan of Hoti (ML)	50.5
Utmannama	Abdul Aziz Khan (Cong)	58.9
Razzar	Manfatullah Khan (Cong)	73.6
Amazai	Qazi Attaullah Khan (Cong)	62.8
Hangu	Syed Ali Badshah (Cong)	57.9
Kohat	Pir Shahinshah (Cong)	51.3
Teri South	Sahib Gul (Cong)	51.9
Teri North	Muhd Aslam Khan (Cong)	49.4
Bannu East	Muhd Yakub Khan (Cong)	81.2
Bannu West	Akbar Ali Khan (Cong)	68.8
Lakki East	Habibullah Khan (ML)	55.5
Lakki West	Pir Abdul Latif Khan (ML)	57.0

continued

Table 3.2 continued

Constituency	Name and Party of Successful Candidate	Percentage of the Total Vote
Tank	Qutbauddin Khan Nawab of Tank (ML)	48.7
Kulachi	Sardar Asadullah Jan Khan (Ju)*	65.9
Dera Ismail Khan South	Nawabzada Allah Nawaz Khan (Ju)*	59.4
Dera Ismail Khan North	Abdullah Khan (Cong)	NA

*Ju = Jamiat-ul-Ulema-i-Hind
Source: Compiled from *Return Showing Results of Elections to the Central Legislative Assembly and Provincial Assemblies in 1945-6*, New Delhi, 1948, p. 208 and ff.

Table 3.3: Punjab Provincial Assembly Results 1946

Constituency	Name and Party of Successful Candidate	Percentage of the Total Vote
MUHAMMADAN URBAN		
Southern Towns	Khwaja Ghulam Samad (ML)	97.9
South Eastern Towns	Shaukat Hayat Khan (ML)	78.6
Eastern Towns	Malik Barkat Ali (ML)	83.3
Inner Lahore	Wazir Mohammad (ML)	87.1
Outer Lahore	Mohd Rafiq (ML)	99.0
Amritsar City	Sheikh Sadiq Hassan (ML)	65.1
North Eastern Towns	Sheikh Karakat Ali (ML)	61.9
Rawalpindi Division Towns	Firoz Khan Noon (ML)	86.2
Multan Division Towns	Sheikh Mohd Ameen (ML)	75.7
MUHAMMADAN RURAL		
Hissar	Ch. Sahib Dad Khan (ML)	76.7
Rohtak	Mohd Khurshaid Khan (ML)	83.8
North West Gurgaon	Maulvi Ahmad Jan (ML)	47.5
South East Gurgaon	Mahtab Khan (ML)	45.8
Karnal	Sufi Abdul Hamid Khan (ML)	87.9
Ambala and Simla	Mohd Hassan Khan (ML)	85.3
Kangra and Eastern Hoshiarpur	Ali Akbar Khan (ML)	66.5
Hoshiarpur West	Rana Nasrullah Khan (ML)	46.8
Jullundur North	Mohd Abdus Salam (ML)	72.6
Jullundur South	Wali Mohammad (ML)	57.8
Ludhiana	Mohd. Iqbal Ahmad Khan (ML)	68.2
Ferozepore Central	Nawab of Mamdot (ML)	56.2
Ferozepore East	Mian Bashir Ahmad (ML)	70.0
Fazilka	Bagh Ali (Unionist)	61.9
Lahore	Muzaffar Ali Khan Qizilbash (Unionist)	53.6
Chunian	Sardar Muhd Hussain (ML)	77.7
Kasur	Mian Iftikhar-ud-din (ML)	74.4
Amritsar	Nasrullah Khan (ML)	69.9
Tarn Taran	Ch. Akram Ali Khan (ML)	58.8
Ajnala	Ch. Zafarullah Khan (ML)	73.8
Gurdaspur East	Ch. Ghulam Farid (ML)	93.7
Batala	Ch. Fateh Mohd Sial (ML)	38.9
Shakargarh	Ch. Abdul Ghafoor (ML)	50.3
Sialkot North	Ch. Nasir Din (ML)	73.9
Sialkot South	Mian Mumtaz Daultana (ML)	64.5

continued

Table 3.3 continued

Constituency	Name and Party of Successful Candidate	Percentage of the Total Vote
Gujranwala North	Ch. Salah-ud-din (ML)	55.4
Gujranwala East	Ch. Zafarullah Khan (ML)	50.8
Hafizabad	Ch. Raj Muhammad (ML)	72.3
Sheikhupura	Ch. Mohammad Hussain (ML)	76.9
Nankana Sahib	Rai Shahadat Khan (ML)	53.4
Shahdara	Ch. Roshin Din (ML)	75.9
Gujrat North	Ch. Fazal Ilahi (ML)	70.0
Gujrat East	Ch. Asghar Ali (Unionist)	66.5
South East Gujrat	Ch. Bahawal Bakhsh (ML)	82.5
North West Gujrat	Ch. Jahan Khan (ML)	73.7
South West Gujrat	Ch. Ghulam Rasul (ML)	70.2
Shahpur	Khizr Hayat Khan Tiwana (Unionist)	56.6
Bhalwal	K.B. Sheikh Fazal Haq Piracha (ML)	57.9
Sargodha	Allah Bakhsh Khan Tiwana (Unionist)	53.1
Jhelum	Raja Khair Mehti Khan (ML)	81.9
Pind Dadan Khan	Raja Ghazanfar Ali Khan (ML)	72.9
Chakwal	Raja Muhd Sarfraz Ali Khan (ML)	71.1
Rawalpindi Sadar	Ch. Zafar-ul-Haq (ML)	53.9
Gujar Khan	Raja Said Akbar Khan (ML)	91.9
Rawalpindi East	Raja Kala Khan (ML)	83.7
Attock North	Sardar Mumtaz Ali Khan (ML)	50.9
Attock Central	Muhd Shah Nawaz Khan (Unionist)	unopposed
Attock South	Pir Makhad (Unionist)	66.4
Mianwali North	Khan Abdul Sattar Khan (ML)	67.1
Mianwali South	Muhd Abdullah Khan (Unionist)	50.7
Montgomery	NA (ML)	83.5
Okara	Mian Abdul Haq (ML)	87.9
Dipalpur	Syed Ashiq Hussain (ML)	68.3
Pakpattan	Rana Abdul Hamid Khan (ML)	63.2
Lyallpur	Ch. Aziz Din (ML)	75.9
Samundri	Mir Mohd Khan (ML)	63.2
Toba Tek Singh	Mian Nurullah (ML)	52.3
Jaranwala	Rai Anwar Khan (ML)	65.9
Jhang East	Syed Ghulam Mohd Shah (ML)	unopposed
Jhang Central	Syed Mubarik Ali Shah (ML)	75.6
Jhang West	Mehr Muhd Arif Khan (ML)	90.2

continued

APPENDIX C   131

Table 3.3 continued

Constituency	Name and Party of Successful Candidate	Percentage of the Total Vote
Multan	Nawab Ashiq Hussain (Unionist)	52.2
Shujabad	Syed Reza Shah Gilani (ML)	61.6
Lodhran	Ghulam Mustafa Shah Gilani (ML)	77.5
Mailsi	Allah Yar Khan Daultana (ML)	75.5
Khanewal	Syed Budhari Shah (ML)	71.1
Kabirwala	Syed Nan Bahar Shah (ML)	69.4
Muzaffargarh Sadar	K.S. Abdul Hameed Khan (ML)	60.3
Alipur	Mian Muhd Ibrahim Barq (Unionist)	46.1
Muzaffargarh North	Mian Mohd Ghulam Gurmani	66.8
Dera Ghazi Khan North	Sardar Attar Muhd Khan (ML)	unopposed
Dera Ghazi Khan Central	K.B. Faiz Muhd Khan (Unionist)	55.0
Dera Ghazi Khan South	K.B. Sardar Dreshak (ML)	34.3

Source: Compiled and calculated from *Return Showing the Results of the Elections to the Central Legislative Assembly and the Provincial Legislatures 1945-6*, New Delhi, 1948.

APPENDIX D
Biographical Notes of Leading Muslim Leaguers

SHAMSUDDIN AHMED (1889-1969)

Native of the Nadia District of East Bengal. Graduated with LL.B. from Presidency College, Calcutta. Joined Calcutta High Court as an advocate in 1917. Participated in 1919 Non-Co-operation Movement. Secretary of Provincial Khilafat Committee and Bengal Provincial Congress 1921-5. Congress Representative of Bengal Legislative Council from 1927-9. Commissioner of Calcutta Corporation 1933-6. Joined Fazlul Huq's Krishak Praja Movement. Elected to Bengal Legislative Council for Krishak Praja Party. Member of first and second Fazlul Huq coalitions. Joined Muslim League in 1944. Elected as Muslim League candidate for Kushtia in 1946. Member of Suhrawardy's Government 1946-7.

MALIK BARKAT ALI (1885-1946)

Born Lahore. Educated Forman Christian College. LL.B. 1916. Early member of Mian Fazl-i-Husain's 'Progressive' Muslim League. Delegate to Calcutta All-Parties Convention 1928. In the political wilderness 1925-36 as he lacked a rural powerbase. Vice-President of the Reorganized Punjab Muslim League in 1936. One of only two successful Muslim League candidates in 1937. Co-drafter of the Jinnah-Sikander Pact, but violently disagreed with Sikander's interpretation. Opponent of the new Punjab Muslim League created under Unionist tutelage. Patron Punjab Muslim Students Federation 1937-44. Elected as Muslim League candidate for Eastern Towns Constituency in 1946, but died shortly after on 5 April.

MIAN MUMTAZ DAULTANA (1916-)

Educated Government College, Lahore; Corpus Christi Oxford. Called to Bar 1940. On returning to India joined the All-India Muslim League in 1942. Returned as Unionist in bye-election for West Punjab Landholder's seat, following Muhammad Hayat Khan Noon's death in 1943. Despite his family's close links with the Unionist Party, became active Leaguer after Khizr's split with Jinnah in April 1944. General Secretary of Punjab Muslim League, almost immediately afterwards. General Secretary of All-India Muslim League Committee of Action in 1945. Responsible for Punjab League's 'Progressive' manifesto for 1946 elections. Returned for Sialkot South, by this time he had established himself as a dominant figure in the Punjab League.

MOHAMMAD HASHIM GAZDAR

Member of the Silawatas business community of Karachi, ran his own engineering and contracting firm. Rival of Hatim Alavi, a Bohra businessman whom he defeated in the 1934 Karachi Municipal Corporation Election, and later of Yusuf Haroon. Leading member of Sind Azad Party and of the Sind Muslim Parliamentary Board in 1936, until he defected to the Sind United Party in November 1936 and became one of its Secretaries. Elected to Legislative Assembly in 1937. Remained loyal to the Sind United Party after Hidayatullah formed his first ministry. Member of All-India Muslim League Council in 1937-8. Led opposition to the formation of Allah Baksh's ministry in March 1938. Passed over by Mir Bandeh Ali in his Cabinet making. Supported G.M. Sayed in his opposition to Hidayatullah from 1943 onwards. Only split with Sayed shortly before he was expelled from the League. Headed 22-member Organizing Committee of League after Sayed's purge, and took over from him as Sind League President.

ABDULLAH HAROON

Prominent Memon sugar merchant of Karachi. Elected the Sind Muslim League's Vice-President in 1920, also played a prominent role in the Sind Khilafat Committee. Founded *Al-Wahid*, a Sindhi daily, to do propaganda for Khilafat cause. Became President of the Karachi branch of the All-India Muslim Conference in 1931. In 1934 its National President, the Agha Khan, appointed Haroon the Conference's Secretary. Haroon was also elected to the Indian Legislative Assembly in 1934. He also took a leading role in the movement for Sind's separation. Formed the Sind United Party in June 1936. Knighted in January 1937. Defeated in the Karachi City North Muhammadan Urban Constituency in the 1937 provincial elections. Became Vice-President of the Sind Muslim League in March 1938. Also member of Central Legislative Assembly and Muslim League Working Committee. Chairman of the Reception Committee of October 1938 Sind Provincial Muslim League Conference. Elected Sind League President November 1938. Played a leading role in the Manzilgah Mosque agitation in Sukkur in 1939. Criticized Mir Bandeh Ali's ministers for ignoring All-India Muslim League interests. His sudden death in May 1942 robbed Jinnah of a loyal servant. Abdullah Haroon's eldest son, Yusuf, became Sind League Secretary, but was replaced by Sayed in 1944. He thereafter supported Hidayatullah in his struggle with the League President. Played a leading role in the Organizing Committee set up to re-establish the League, after Sayed was purged.

134 APPENDIX D

ABUL HASHIM

Muslim League activist from the Burdwan District of West Bengal. Became Bengal Provincial Muslim Secretary in 1943. Supported by enthusiastic Dacca University students, led campaign to convert local branches of League from paper organizations into a mass organizational base. His democratization of the Dacca League led to conflict with the Muslim League Premier Nazimuddin, and the Muslim League President Maulana Akram Khan. Despite being branded a Communist, he was reconfirmed League Secretary at the November 1944 Calcutta League Council meeting. Elected for Burdwan Constituency in 1946. Supported Suhrawardy and other Unionists in their efforts to prevent Bengal's partition.

GHULAM HUSSAIN HIDAYATULLAH

Born in Kashmir, convert from Hinduism. Represented Sind in the Bombay Legislative Council in the late 1920s. It was during this period that his long-term enmity began with Sir Shahnawaz Bhutto. He played an active role in the Sind Separation Movement. Initially joined Sind United Party, but launched breakaway Sind Muslim Party in November 1936. Though the Sind United Party won a clear majority of Muslim seats, the Governor Graham chose Hidayatullah as Chief Minister. Hidayatullah based his strength in the Assembly on the *Mir-Baluch* bloc. Formed new Sind Democratic Party in January 1938, resigned on 22 March. Joined Sind Muslim League in July 1938, resigned in January 1939 because of his growing rivalry with Abdullah Haroon. Returned to the League fold in October 1942 at the head of a ministry which remained in office until June 1945. Faced growing opposition from the 'Progressive' League President G.M. Sayed. Called upon to be Chief Minister, once more after the 1946 elections. Reckoned in the early 1940s by the British to be 'all against Pakistan'.

MAULANA AKRAM KHAN

Born in the 24-Parganas District of West Bengal. Leading journalist and politician. Founded the pan-Islamic *Muhammadi* in 1903. Secretary of the Anjuman-i-Islam Bengala in 1913. In 1936 launched the *Azad* paper which gave powerful support to Fazl-Huq's Coalition Ministry (1937-41). Despite ill-health was Bengal League President from 1942 until Partition. Supported Nazimuddin in his struggle with Abul Hashim and Suhrawardy. Opposed democratization of League at November 1944 Calcutta Council session, but stayed on as President in compromise agreement. Wanted to retain Calcutta for Pakistan, but prepared to lose Hashim's troublesome Burdwan Division in any Partition. Ensured that his son, Khaizul Anam Khan, was nominated for the Bengal League Working Committee in 1943.

AURANGZEB KHAN

A member of a Gandapur Khani family from Kulachi, N.W.F.P. Practised Law in Peshawar. Elected for N.W.F.P. Landowner's seat as an Independent in 1937, after K.B. Saadullah Khan placed sufficient property in his name to allow him to qualify. Later split with Saadullah Khan who he replaced as League President and caused criminal charges to be brought against. Formed Muslim League ministry in May 1943 which became notorious for its corruption. The conflict between him and Saadullah Khan led to the Provincial League being dissolved on the All-India Committee of Action's recommendation. Whilst the reorganization was still going on his government was brought down on 12 March 1945. Jinnah refused to give Aurangzeb Khan a ticket for the 1946 Provincial Elections, although many of the ex-Premier's supporters received places on the Frontier League's Parliamentary Board.

IFTIKHAR HUSSAIN KHAN, NAWAB OF MAMDOT

Son of Nawab Shah Nawaz Khan, one of the Punjab's leading Pathans and the largest Muslim landholder in the East Punjab. Iftikhar Hussain succeeded him as Nawab in March 1942. Became President of the Punjab Muslim League early in 1943, and was soon more active in its affairs than his father had been. Re-elected League President in December 1944. Active rural propagandist against the Unionist Party. Returned unopposed for the family constituency of Ferozepore Central in 1946. Unable to form a Muslim League Government, despite lengthy negotiations with the Sikh Akalis. Played a leading role in the direct action campaign which brought down the Khizr coalition in March 1947.

RAJA GHAZANFAR ALI KHAN (1895-1963)

Son of Raja Saif Ali Khan, head of the Khokhar Rajputs of the Jhelum District of West Punjab. Uncle of Pir Fazl Shah of Jalalpur Sharif. Minister Alwar State 1927. Member of the Indian Council of States 1933-7. Elected as the Muslim League candidate for Pind Dadan Khan in 1937, but joined the Unionist Party when offered a Parliamentary Secretaryship. Joined Muslim League in 1944, following the collapse of the Khizr-Jinnah Talks. Active rural propagandist, and the League's most eloquent speaker in the Provincial Assembly. Successful Muslim League candidate for Pind Dadan Khan in 1946. Prominent in the Muslim League direct action campaign.

SHAUKAT HAYAT KHAN (1915-)

Son of Sikander Hayat Khan, Unionist Premier of the Punjab from 1937 until his death in December 1942. Served in the Indian Army at the beginning of the Second World War. Elected to Punjab Assembly, shortly after his father's death, and was made Minister for Public Works, despite his political inexperience, in Khizr Hayat Khan Tiwana's Unionist Government. Embarrassed his colleagues by his open support for Pakistan. Dismissed on 26 April 1944 on the eve of the breakdown of the Jinnah-Khizr Talks for alleged 'administrative misconduct'. Active rural propagandist against the Unionists. Elected Deputy Leader of the Punjab League on 2 December 1944. Member of the *Mashaikh* Committee. Elected for South East Towns Muslim Constituency in 1946. Prominent in the 1947 Muslim League direct action campaign.

MOHAMMED AYUB KHUHRO

Landowner from the Larkana District of Sind, member of the Bombay Legislative Council in the mid-1920s, played an active role in the campaign for Sind's separation. Elected as Secretary of the Sind United Party in November 1936, but defected to join Hidayatullah's Sind Muslim Party. Member of the Council of the All-India Muslim League in 1937. President Larkana District Muslim League also in 1937, encouraged spread of League activity there, following the creation of the Allah Baksh Government. Supported Haroon, rather than his earlier mentor, Hidayatullah, as Sind League President in 1938. Played a leading role in the Manzilgah restoration campaign. Became Minister in Mir Bandeh Ali's Government of 1940-1. Became Sind League President on Abdullah Haroon's death. Also in 1943 became Member of All-India Muslim League Working Committee. Opposed Gazdar-Sayed axis in the Sind League. Arrested for a possible hand in Allah Baksh's murder in May 1943, but released in August 1945. Opposed Sayed group in run-up to elections, whilst at the same time intriguing against Hidayatullah.

KHWAJA NAZIMUDDIN (1894-1964)

Member of the Dacca Nawab family. Educated Aligarh, London, Cambridge, Bar-at-Law, but did not take up practice. Chairman of the Dacca Municipality 1922-9. Minister for Education 1929-34. Member of the Bengal Executive Council 1934-7. Home Minister in Fazlul Huq's ministry of 1937-41 when he resigned with the other Muslim League ministers. Member of the All-India Muslim League Working Committee 1937-47. Leader of Muslim League opposition in Assembly January 1942 to March 1943. Muslim League Chief Minister April 1943 to March 1945. Faced growing opposition from Suhrawardy and Abul Hashim, although supported by the League President Maulana Akram Khan. Suhrawardy pushed him to one side, after he secured a majority on the League Parliamentary Board. Elected to Central Legislative Assembly in 1946, and in 1947 to Pakistan Constituent Assembly. Hovered between Divisionists and Unionists over the issue of Bengal's Partition.

ABDUR RAB NISHTAR

Lawyer from Peshawar, was a Frontier Congress leader until his resignation in 1931. Elected as an Independent for the Peshawar city constituency in 1937. Joined Aurangzeb Khan's ministry in 1943 as Finance Minister. Became Jinnah's loyal contact in the Frontier. Struggled for supremacy with Abdul Qaiyum Khan after Aurangzeb did not receive a ticket. Lost his seat in the 1946 elections partly because of his unpopular association with the Aurangzeb ministry, partly because of Abdul Qaiyum's machinations. Increasingly became involved in All-India politics. Jinnah's nominee at the May 1946 Simla Tripartite Conference to discuss the *Cabinet Mission Plan*. Entered the Interim Government as Health Minister in October 1946. One of the Muslim League leaders which met on 3 June 1947 to agree to Mountbatten's Partition Plan. Along with Liaquat, Patel, and Nehru, member of Partition Committee to work out the actual machinery of separation.

FIROZ KHAN NOON (1893-1970)

Member Noon landlord family of the Shahpur District of West Punjab. Entered Punjab Legislative Council in 1921. Minister for Local Government 1927-31, Education 1931-6. Indian High Commissioner in London 1936-41. Member Viceroy's Executive Council 1941, became the first Indian to hold the Defence Portfolio in 1942. Member of the Imperial War Council 1944. Left the Viceroy's Council in 1945, after the collapse of the Simla Conference. Campaigned for the Punjab Muslim League against the Unionists. Elected as League candidate for Rawalpindi Division Towns Constituency in 1946. Arrested in Lahore, along with his English wife, Vicky, during the direct action campaign of 1947.

ABDUL QAYUM KHAN

Kashmiri barrister. He served as the Congress' Deputy Leader in the Central Assembly from 1938-45. After prolonged secret negotiations he joined the League on 16 August 1945, just days before the Viceroy ordered new elections. He was the most prominent Congressman to switch allegiances. Elected Convenor of the Frontier League's Election Board, a position he used to deny his rivals tickets. He rose rapidly to prominence as he stood outside the factional groupings which were paralysing the Frontier League. He secured his election and Nishtar's defeat in the Peshawar City Dual Constituency by secretly getting his supporters to cast both ballots for him. He was thus unchallenged as the Leader of the Frontier Muslim League Assembly Party.

G.M. SAYED

Matiari Syed landowner from the Dadu District of Sind. Member of the Bombay Legislative Council during the 1920s and active in the Sind

Separation Movement. Earlier member Sind Khilafat Committee. Member of the Sind United Party in 1936. Resigned from this in March 1938 to join Hidayatullah's Sind Democratic Party. Organized his own bloc of *Sayed* supporters in the Assembly. Shifted support for a short time to Allah Baksh, but gravitated towards the Muslim League as Baksh strengthened his ties with the Congress. Joined League early in 1938. Took an active role in the Manzilgah campaign, during which he was arrested. Became a Member of Mir Bandeh Ali's Government of 1940-1. In 1943 became Member of All-India Muslim League Working Committee and President of the Sind League. In July 1944 he called on Hidayatullah and the other ministers to resign. Supported for a while by Gazdar in his struggle against the ministers. Intrigued to bring down the Muslim League Government in February 1943. When he was reduced to a minority position on the Sind Parliamentary Board, ran 'progressive' League candidates against the official candidates. Expelled from the League early in January 1946, but returned to the Assembly with a sizeable group of supporters. Argued for agrarian reform and the creation of a 'Sindhi Pakistan'.

SHEIKH ABDUL MAJID SINDHI

Born into influential Lilaram Hindu family of Thatta Sind, but converted during his youth to Islam. Editor of G.M. Bhurgari's newspaper *Al-Amin*. Later took over from Bhurgari, leadership of Sind Separation Movement. Secretary of the Sind Khilafat Committee. Founded the Sind Azad Party in Karachi in 1935. Member of Muslim League's Sind Parliamentary Board in 1936, but held back from fully merging the Azad Party with the League. Scored a notable success in the 1937 elections when he defeated the Sind United Party leader Sir Shahnawaz Bhutto in his native Larkana Constituency. Joined Hidayatullah's Sind Muslim Party in the Assembly after the elections. Member All-India Muslim League Council 1937-8. In early February 1938 became President of the Sind Provincial League, helped establish its local branches. Defeated by Abdullah Haroon in election for post of President in November 1938. Played an active role in Manzilgah campaign. Minister in Mir Bandeh Ali's Government 1941-2. Drifted out of the League for a short time in 1944 when he allied himself with Moula Baksh's Azad group.

HUSSAIN SHAHEED SUHRAWARDY (1892-1963)

Born in Midnapore, West Bengal. Educated at St. Xavier's College, Calcutta and Oxford. Father Judge in Calcutta High Court. Entered politics through the Calcutta Corporation. Was Deputy Mayor under C.R. Das's patronage in 1923. Gained an important base of support in the Bengal National Chamber of Labour. Entered Bengal Legislative Council in 1924. Earlier had played a leading role in the Bengal Khilafat

Conference. Active in the United Muslim Party which merged with the Muslim League in 1936. Became League Secretary. Minister in Fazlul Huq's 1937-41 Government. Resigned in December 1941 after earlier organizing demonstrations against Huq's breaking with the All-India Muslim League over membership of the Viceroy's Defence Council. Minister for Civil Supply during the Bengal famine in Nazimuddin's 1943-5 ministry. Increasingly at odds with the Dacca Old Guard, relied on his strength within the League organization to counteract Nazimuddin's Assembly strength. Ensured himself the Chief Ministership when he gained control of the Bengal Parliamentary Board and shortly after dissolved the Election Fund and Provincial Propaganda Committees. Chief Minister 1946-7. Worked for a sovereign, united Bengal State, but Partition became increasingly inevitable after the great Calcutta killing of 16 August. Jinnah prevented him from forming a coalition with the Congress in April and September 1946. Had fruitless negotiations with Sarat Bose and Kiran Shankar Roy in May 1947. Remained in West Bengal at the time of Partition.

The Press and The Muslim League in the 'Pakistan Areas'

The press was an important weapon in the Muslim League's struggle for Pakistan. Newspapers carried Punjabi and Bengali *Pirs'* appeals to voters in the 1946 elections. They were frequently the only source of information on Muslim League meetings and resolutions for the population at large. The Muslim League press's highlighting of the corruption of Hindu contractors during the Second World War and its repeated attacks on the Unionist Government's handling of the civil supply situation played an important role in swinging opinion in its favour in the 'cornerstone' of Pakistan.

It is important to note at this point that in a semi-literate society recorded circulation figures for newspapers are likely to greatly underestimate the number of people influenced by newspaper reporting. The practice is still quite widespread today in Pakistan of reading aloud a newspaper to illiterate villagers and townspeople. The press was thus an effective channel for reaching large numbers of Muslims along with more 'traditional' forms of communication—the use of fairs and *Urs* ceremonies to spread the message by word of mouth. The impact of press reporting can be seen in the large crowds which flocked to Jinnah whenever he visited the Majority areas. Many of those who attended his meetings had never seen him before nor were able to understand what he said. But they had built up an intense loyalty to him through his constant depiction in the Muslim newspapers as the living symbol of their community's regeneration.

Although the Muslim League had significant press support by the final stages of the Pakistan Movement, it was an uphill struggle. It lagged far behind the Congress in financial resources and journalistic expertise.[1] Whilst the Congress point of view had been put forward in Punjab by the *Tribune* from the 1880s, on the eve of Partition the Muslim League still did not have an English daily paper in that region. *Dawn* had been launched as its main All-India organ in 1942. But as a Punjabi Leaguer wrote to Jinnah, 'In the particular circumstances in which we find ourselves in Lahore, it is necessary that the Muslim League organ should reflect as well as guide the opinion in the Punjab and this can be adequately done only when the paper's editorials are conceived, inspired, influenced, and written in the atmosphere of Lahore. This work cannot be done from Delhi'.[2] Jinnah ruled out on financial grounds, however, the idea of issuing a Lahore edition of

Dawn. The best that could be done was to convert a previously pro-Unionist daily, the *Eastern Times*. It could not always be relied upon to follow the official League line in its editorial policy.[3] Other 'sympathetic' Muslim papers displayed similar alarming independence from the League hierarchy's viewpoint.[4] They frequently became involved in the faction fights of their wealthy proprietors, thus adding to the divisions in the League's ranks in the Majority areas rather than providing a unifying influence. The Sindhi daily, *Al-Wahid*, was a good case in point. It was founded and funded by the Haroons. Almost inevitably it was drawn into the conflict which raged between Yusuf Haroon and the Sind League President G.M. Sayed from late May 1944 onwards.

Within Punjab, the Muslim League not only faced strong press opposition from the Congress, but also from the Unionists. During the early 1940s, they ensured favourable coverage from certain Urdu newspapers such as *Inqilab*, *Shahbaz*, and *Ehsan* by providing them with lavish subsidies. A particularly successful way of influencing a newspaper was by providing lucrative government advertising. As the struggle intensified between the Unionists and the Muslim League, many Urdu papers switched their allegiance to the latter. So that by 1946 in the Urdu if not the English language press, the Muslim League had powerful support. The Nawab of Mamdot, for example, secured control of the Urdu weekly *Jatistan* in 1944, changed its name to *Pakistan* and converted it into a pro-League paper. *Shahbaz* underwent a similar transformation as did *Vakil*, which was revived in October 1945. Some papers still remained loyal to the Unionists as for example the *Yadava Zamindar*, an Urdu weekly published in Gurgaon, and the Urdu bi-weekly *Rajput Gazette*.

The Punjab League's supporters not only secured existing Urdu papers, but funded new enterprises. The most important of these initiatives was the establishment of *Nawa-e-Waqt*. This started life as a small-sized fortnightly within a week of the passing of the *Lahore Resolution*. Its patron and editor were Mian Bashir Ahmad and Hameed Nizami. The paper's early cultural emphasis gradually gave way to an open political stance in favour of Pakistan. In 1942 *Nawa-e-Waqt* became a daily under Hameed Nizami's proprietorship. It devoted itself to the League's struggle with the Unionists and was not slow to criticize those Punjabi Leaguers who did not adopt a 'progressive' and fully 'Islamic' attitude in this conflict. The paper's influence extended far further than indicated by its meagre circulation figures.[5]

Whilst *Nawa-e-Waqt* was the most prominent Urdu paper to support the Muslim League, other more local publications also deserve mention. These include such papers as *Khayyam*, a weekly published from Lahore, and *Ailan*, a Jullundur weekly. Periodicals founded as community papers[6] also carried sympathetic reports of League activities, typical of these was the Urdu weekly *Muslim Rajput*. Finally, reference must be made to *Zamindar*, which under Zafar Ali Khan's guidance had earlier been the main voice of the Khilafat and Pan-Islamic Movements within Punjab.

Vernacular press support for the Congress came from National Congress, an Urdu daily, from the Delhi based *Hindustan,* and intermittently from *Milap* and *Pratap.* The latter was published daily in both Urdu and Hindi but reflected the views of the Hindu Mahasabha rather than the Congress. The *Desh Bhaghat* and *Arorbans Sudharak* similarly stood for the Mahasabha's views, whilst at the same time supporting the more communal elements within the Punjab Congress. Like *Pratap,* they were closely associated with the Arya Samaj. None of these vernacular, communally oriented papers possessed the same influence as *Tribune.* Its daily circulation of 26,500 copies in 1945-6 dwarfed the sales of all other papers in Punjab. Only the *Civil and Military Gazette* (15,020) with its predominantly European readership remotely approached this figure. The *Eastern Times,* for example, sold just two and a half thousand copies, as did *Nawa-e-Waqt.* Although as we have seen earlier, such papers' influence were far more extensive than this.

There were also delays and difficulties in establishing papers sympathetic to the Muslim League in Sind. A Muslim League English daily was not launched until December 1945.[7] The new paper called *The Sind Times* was started by a Karachi advocate to counter the attacks which were then being made on the League by the *Muslim Voice.* A weekly English League paper called *Al-Jamiat* published from Shikarpur had come into existence only a matter of months before *The Sind Times.* The large Gujarati speaking community of Karachi was no better served with Muslim League literature than their English counterparts.

Almost on the eve of Partition, in October 1946, the first pro-League Gujarati daily entitled *Zulfikar* appeared on the streets. Another latecomer was *Hilal-e-Pakistan,* a Sindhi daily from Hyderabad which was first published the following month.

There were of course more established vernacular papers which gave their support to the Muslim League.[8] One of these was *Baluchistan-e-Jadid,* founded in 1933. This Urdu morning daily, edited by Muhammad Nasim Talvi, had a relatively large circulation in both Sind and Baluchistan. It was overshadowed, however, by *Al-Wahid.* This Sindhi daily had established its reputation during the Khilafat period. During the early 1940s *Al-Wahid* served as the Sind Muslim League's official organ. But after Yusuf Haroon's exclusion from the post of General Secretary by G.M. Sayed, it was converted into an independent paper, with Sheikh Abdul Majid as Chairman of a Board of Directors which included both Khuhro and Yusuf Haroon. The paper became increasingly critical of Sayed, the League President. The latter used the columns of another Sindhi daily, *Qubarni,* to put forward his views in the fierce faction fight.

The Nationalist press splashed across its pages the divisions which rent the Sind Muslim League in 1945-6. The most vocal and influential of the League's opponents was the *Sind Observer*. This paper was published in Karachi and founded by Sindhi Hindu businessmen. In the early 1930s it had mounted a persistent campaign against Sind's separation from the Bombay Presidency. Later it supported both Allah and Moula Baksh's nationalist activities, whilst highlighting the Muslim League's Sayed-Mir divisions. Non-Hindu papers also attacked it for its 'unpatriotic' and communal stance. Most notable among these were the *Karachi Daily* and the *Sansar Samachar*.

Although Bengali Muslim journalism lagged behind the Hindu press, it predated advances in other 'Pakistan regions' and contributed to a mini renaissance. Sir Shamsul Huda (1862-1922), a Calcutta-based lawyer, started a Bengali weekly *Sudhakar* in November 1889. In addition, he financed *The Muhammadan Observer* which when it was established in 1880 was the first English weekly in Bengal to be owned by a Muslim. The *Muhammadi* was another early Muslim paper. This was founded by Haji Abdullah, a Bihari businessman, in 1905 and later under Maulana Akram Khan's editorship followed a strong pan-Islamist line. During the Khilafat campaign two short-lived dailies *Savik* (Bengali) and *Zamana* (Urdu) were published from the office of the *Muhammadi*. The latter paper was converted from a monthly to a weekly by its new owner Maulana Akram Khan. He also started a monthly periodical entitled *Islam* in 1916. His most important journalistic activities, however, centred round the Bengali daily *Azad* which he founded in 1936. All the Bengal League's circulars were published through its columns. *Azad* gave powerful support to Fazlul Huq's coalition ministry (1937-41). Thereafter, it acted as Khwaja Nazimuddin's mouthpiece. Abul Hashim complained bitterly about its blind support for the ministerialist group. His statements were frequently censored before appearing in its pages.

The leading Urdu Muslim League paper *Asr-e-jadid* more successfully steered clear of the factional rivalries within the Bengal League. It had been founded in 1920 by a Deobandi scholar, Maulana Sheikh Ahmed Osmani. He used the paper as a vehicle for his attacks on the pro-Congress views of the *Jamiat-ul-Ulema-i-Hind*. The *Star of India* and the *Morning News* were the two main English language pro-League dailies. Like *Azad* they supported the ministerialists in their struggle with Abul Hashim and the 'progressives' The *Morning News* had been founded in August 1932 by Abdur Rahman Siddiqui and Khwaja Nooruddin. A.K. Ghaznavi had almost simultaneously launched *Star of India* as a successor to the *Calcutta Evening News*.

Press support for the Muslim League in the North-West Frontier Province was much weaker than in Bengal. This reflected the long period of dominance by the *Khudai Khidmatgars*, Muslim educational backwardness and the League's peripheral position in Frontier society. The Haji of Turangzai's movement during the first decade of the twentieth century had encouraged a Pushtu literary revival which had later been channelled into nationalist politics by the *Anjuman-i-islah-ul-*

Afghania. Significantly the newly emerging Pushtu press supported the *Khudai Khidmatgars*, whilst the Muslim League had to rely on Urdu newspapers. None of these, however, approached the influence of the *Pakhtun*[9] journal of the Khan brothers. Moreover, they also had to compete with the Urdu *Frontier Advocate* paper of Amir Chand Bombwal and the *Sarhadi Samachar* of Mehr Chand Khanna[10] which represented the Frontier Hindus' opinion. The main Urdu pro-League papers were *Al-Jamiat Sarhad, Al-Falah, Shura,* and *Sarhad.* They depicted Frontier Congressmen as traitors to Islam and uncovered evidence of alleged communal bias in the first Khan Sahib ministry of 1937-9. Their anti-Congress propaganda was reinforced by personal attacks which were often libellous on its leaders.[11] The vernacular League papers were also almost inevitably drawn into the factional rivalries and charges of corruption which punctuated the two years of Aurangzeb Khan's period in office. The English language *Khyber Mail* was, however, more restrained in its editorial comment throughout this period. It was a Peshawar-based weekly which began publication in 1932. Whilst being sympathetic to the Muslim League, it was never an official League organ.

The uneven development of a Muslim League press in the 'Pakistan Areas' reflected the halting character of its growth in political organization. The predominance of a few centres of publication—Calcutta, Delhi, Lahore, Peshawar, Karachi—also revealed in microcosm the League's experience of urban concentration. The press also mirrors the League's reliance on 'influential' supporters and the intense factional rivalry which followed from this. On the other hand, the increase in new titles from 1942 onwards bears witness to a growing Muslim self-confidence and will to achieve Pakistan. The press helped to channel this by building up loyalty to Jinnah's symbolic leadership. It also assisted traditional methods of communication in the spread of the Muslim League's message to the rural voters.

REFERENCE

1. The Sindhi Muslim Leaguer Hatim Alavi wrote to Jinnah in November 1944 suggesting that scholarships should be set up to send 20 Muslims annually to either America, England or Australia to receive training in English journalism. Alavi to Jinnah, 13 November 1944, SHC Sind 2:63.
2. Ahmed Shafi to Jinnah, 30 October 1944, SHC General Correspondence, Punjab, Vol. 1.
3. Ibid.
4. A. Haye to Jinnah, 12 December 1945, SHC General Correspondence, Punjab, Vol. 1.
5. According to the *Statement on Newspapers and Periodicals Published in Punjab* in 1945-6, Lahore, 1946, it daily sold just 2,500 copies.
6. The Jat, Rajput, Gujjar, and Meo Muslim communities all published their own papers, as did the Ahmadi sect; the Sikhs also produced a large number, as did the Hindu, Brahmin, Saini, and Arora castes.

7. *The Daily Gazette*, which had earlier been the unofficial organ of the Sind United Party, did favourably report on the Muslim League's activities during the early 1940s.
8. The Muslim Urdu papers *Islah* and *Hayat*, for example, although they were not official League organs, adopted a broadly pro-League stance.
9. This journal used the royal Afghan emblem on its cover until 1930.
10. Khanna was a banker and large urban landlord. He controlled the Frontier Hindu Sabha and by the early 1940s had emerged as the region's dominant Hindu politician.
11. Rittenberg, op. cit., 1977, p. 290.

Select Bibliography

UNPUBLISHED SOURCES

Private Papers

Chelmsford Papers, India Office Library, London, MSS.EUR E264.
F.L.Brayne Papers, India Office Library, London, MSS.EUR F152.
Halifax Papers, India Office Library, London, MSS.EUR C125.
Linlithgow Papers, India Office Library, London, MSS.EUR F125.
Mian Fazl-i-Husain Papers, India Office Library, London, MSS.EUR E352.
Quaid-i-Azam Papers, National Archives of Pakistan, Islamabad.
Syed Shamsul Hasan Collection, Karachi, Pakistan.

Government Records

India Office Library, London.
National Archives of India, New Delhi.
Records of the Political and Secret Department, 1928-47, L/P&S/10; L/P&S/12; L/P&S/20.
Records of the Public and Judicial Department, 1929-47, L/P&J/5; L/P&J/6; L/P&J/7; and L/P&J/9.
Records of the Military Department, 1940-2, L/Mil/14.
Records of the Home Department (Political) of the Government of India, 1927-45.

All-India Muslim League Records

All-India Muslim League Committee of Action Meetings 1944-7.
All-India Muslim League Working Committee Meetings 1932-7.
Freedom Movement Archives, Karachi.
The Baluchistan Muslim League.
The Bengal Provincial Muslim League.
The North-West Frontier Province Muslim League.
The Punjab Muslim League.
The Sind Provincial Muslim League.

Theses

Jones, A.K., 'Muslim Politics and the Growth of the Muslim League in Sind, 1935-41', Ph.D., thesis, Duke University, 1977.
Rittenberg, S.A., 'The Independence Movement in India's North-West Frontier Province, 1901-47', Ph.D., thesis, Columbia University, 1977.

PUBLISHED SOURCES

Official Publications

Government of Bombay, *Gazetteer of Sind,* Vol. B, Bombay, 1918.
Government of India, *Census of India, 1931,* Delhi, 1933.
———, *Census of India, 1941,* Delhi, 1943.
———, *Return Showing the Results of the Elections in India 1937,* Delhi, 1937.
———, *Return Showing the Results of Elections to the Central Legislative Assembly and the Provincial Legislatures 1945-6,* New Delhi, 1948.
Government of the Punjab, *Gazetteer of the Peshawar District 1897-8,* Lahore, 1898.
Government of Sind, *Hari Report: Minute of Dissent,* Karachi, 1948.
Government of West Pakistan, *West Pakistan Gazetteer: The Former Province of Sind,* Karachi, 1968.
Great Britain, *Report of the Indian Statutory Commission* [Simon], London, 1930.

Newspapers

Civil and Military Gazette, Lahore, 1936-47.
Dawn, Delhi, 1943-6.
Eastern Times, Lahore, 1943-6.
Khyber Mail, Peshawar, 1944-6.
Nawa-i-Waqt, Lahore, 1945-6.
Star of India, Calcutta, 1943-6.
Tribune, Ambala, 1936-44; 1944-6.

Annuals

The Indian Annual Register, Mitra, N.N. (editor), 1944-7, Calcutta.

PRINTED SECONDARY WORKS

Afzal, M. Rafique (editor), *Speeches and Statements of the Quaid-i-Azam Mohammad Ali Jinnah 1911-34 and 1947-48,* Lahore, 1966.
———, (editor), *Malik Barkat Ali: His Life and Writings,* Lahore, 1969.
Ahmad, I. (editor), *Caste and Social Stratification Amongst the Muslims,* Delhi, 1973.
Ahmad, W. (editor), *Diary and Notes of Mian Fazl-i-Husain,* Lahore, 1976.
Alavi, Hamza, 'Kinship in West Punjab Villages', in *Contributions to Indian Sociology,* NS 6, December 1972.
Ali, Chaudhri Mahammed, *The Emergence of Pakistan,* Lahore, 1973.
Baxter, Craig, 'The People's Party *Versus* the Punjab Feudalists', in Korsen H. (editor), *Contemporary Problems of Pakistan,* Leiden, 1976.

Begg, W.D., *The Big Five of Sufism in India*, Ajmer, 1972.
Brass, P., *Language, Religion and Politics in North India*, Cambridge, 1974.
Broomfield, J.H., *Elite Conflict in a Plural Society: Twentieth Century Bengal*, Berkeley, 1968.
Burton, Richard E., *Sindh and the Races that Inhabit the Valley of the Indus*, Karachi, 1968.
Caroe, O., *The Pathans*, London, 1965.
Chatterjee, Partha, 'Bengal Politics and the Muslim Masses 1920-47', in *The Journal of Commonwealth and Comparative Politics*, XX, March 1982.
Douie, J., *The Punjab, North-West Frontier Province and Kashmir*, London, 1932.
Dundas, J.L., *Essayez, The Memoirs of Laurence, Second Marquis of Zetland*, London, 1956.
Gilmartin, D., 'Religious Leadership and the Pakistan Movement in the Punjab', in *Modern Asian Studies*, 13, 3, 1979.
Gordon, L.A., *Bengal: The Nationalist Movement 1876-1940*, London, 1974.
———,'Divided Bengal: Problems of Nationalism and Identity in the 1947 Partition', in *Journal of Comparative Culture and Society*, XV, July 1978.
Hardy, P., *The Muslims of British India*, Cambridge, 1972.
Hasan, M., *Nationalism and Communal Politics in India 1916-28*, New Delhi, 1979.
Husain, A., *Mian Fazl-i-Husain: A Political Biography*, London, 1966.
Jalal, A., *The Sole Spokesman: Jinnah, The Muslim League and the Demand for Pakistan*, Cambridge, 1985.
Jannson, E., *India, Pakistan or Pakhtunistan?*, Uppsala, 1981.
Khaliquzzaman, C., *Pathway to Pakistan*, Lahore, 1961.
Low, D.A. (editor), *Soundings in Modern South Asian History*, London, 1968.
Minault, Gail, *The Khilafat Movement, Religious Symbolism and Political Mobilization in India*, New York, 1982.
Moon, P., *Divide and Quit*, London, 1961.
———,(editor), *Wavell: The Viceroy's Journal*, London, 1973.
———,(editor) with Mansergh, N. and Lumby, E.W.R., *The Transfer of Power 1942-7*, 11 volumes, HMSO, 1970-82.
Nath, R.N., 'Punjab Agrarian Laws and their Economic and Constitutional Bearings', in *The Modern Review*, 1939.
Page, D., *Prelude to Partition: The Indian Muslims and the Imperial System of Control 1920-32*, Oxford, 1982.
Patwardhan, A. and Mehta, A., *The Communal Triangle in India*, Allahabad, 1941.
Philips, C.H. and Wainwright, M. (editors), *The Partition of India: Policies and Perspectives 1935-47*, London, 1970.
Pirzada, S. Sharifuddin, *Foundations of Pakistan*, 2 vols., Karachi, 1970.

150   SELECT BIBLIOGRAPHY

Rizvi, G., *Linlithgow and India—A Study of British Policy and the Political Impasse in India 1936-43*, London, 1978.
Robinson, Frances, *Separatism Among Indian Muslims—The Politics of the United Provinces' Muslims 1936-43*, London, 1978.
Sayeed, K.B., *Pakistan—The Formative Phase*, Karachi, 1960.
Sen, Shila, *Muslim Politics in Bengal: 1937-47*, New Delhi, 1976.
Spain, James, *The Pathan Borderland*, The Hague, 1963.
Talbot, I.A., 'The Growth of the Muslim League in the Punjab 1937-46', in *The Journal of Commonwealth and Comparative Politics*, XX, 1, March 1982.
———, 'The 1946 Punjab Elections', in *Modern Asian Studies*, 14, 1, 1980.
Trevaskis, H.K., *The Land of the Five Rivers*, Oxford, 1928.
Tendulkar, G.D., *Abdul Ghaffar Khan*, Bombay, 1967.
Woodruff, Philip, *The Men Who Ruled India*, 2 vols., New York, 1954.
Zaidi, Z.H. (editor), *M.A. Jinnah—Ispahani Correspondence*, Karachi, 1976.
Zaman, Mukhtar, *Students' Role in the Pakistan Movement*, Karachi, 1978.
Zutshi, G.L., *Frontier Gandhi*, Delhi, 1970.

Glossary

Ahrar	'The Free'. Punjabi Muslim Political Party founded in 1931 by Mazhur Ali Khan and Maulana Ataullah Shah Bukhari
Akhand	United
Anjuman	Association
Azad	Free, independent
Badmashes	Bad characters
Biraderi	'Brotherhood', patrilineal kinship group
Fatwa	Formal judicial decree by a learned religious figure
Hari	Tenant-at-will, landless cultivator
Hijrat	Flight, exodus of Muslims for religious purposes
Jagir	A revenue free land grant for military or political service
Kisan	Peasant
Krishak	Peasant or cultivator
Lakh	One hundred thousand
Lambardar	Village headman
Maulana	A Muslim scholar learned in the Qur'an
Mir	A Baluchi chief or leader in Sind
Murid	A Sufi's disciple
Pakhtunwali	Pathans' system of rules; social code
Parajamba	Factionalism amongst Pathans
Pir	A Muslim saint, spiritual guide
Praja	Tenant
Quaid-i-Azam	'The Great Leader'. Title given to Mohammad Ali Jinnah
Rabi	The spring harvest
Sajjada Nashin	Literally one who sits on the prayer rug; custodian of a Sufi shrine
Satyagraha	Civil Disobedience campaign
Sufi	Muslim mystic. The word comes from 'Suf—wool, the woollen garment worn by early Muslim mystics
Tabur	Literally first cousin. An enemy amongst one's close patrilineal cousins
Taburwali	Rivalry between close kin
Tehsildar	Officer in charge of a Tehsil, a revenue subdivision of a district
Ulema	Singular *Alim*. Persons versed in Islamic religious sciences

Vakil	Advocate or lawyer
Wadero	Chief or large landowner in Sind
Zaildar	Officer in charge of a group of villages
Zamindar	Loosely used to refer to any landowner; strictly speaking a landowner responsible for paying land revenue to the government

Index